Ancestral Voices Spirit is Eternal

Ancestral Voices Spirit is Eternal
Dalian Y Adofo

Foreword by Robin Walker

2016
Printed by CreateSpace, An Amazon.com Company

www.ancestralvoices.co.uk

Calise
Seek within the traditions for what is useful
Its not shameful
Its the same that built ancient civilisations so powerful
SANKOFA
07/10/2016

Copyright © 2016 Dalian Y Adofo

All rights reserved. No part of this publication should be reproduced in any form, stored in a retrieval system, or transmitted by any means, whether electronic or mechanical, without the prior permission in writing from the Author. It is not permissible to be otherwise circulated in any form of binding or cover other than that the current cover. Kindly purchase only authorised editions and not encourage the proliferation of electronic piracy of copyrighted items. Parties interested in the educational use of this material in institutions and workshops should send all enquiries to dalian.adofo@longbelly.co.uk

Cover Design by Dalian Y Adofo

Dedications
To the memories of

Felicia Ama Agyekumwaah Adofo (1943 - 2015)
My dearest mother, first teacher and role model. My eternal gratitude for being a pillar of strength and inspiration.
Damirifa Due

Max Gesner Beauvoir (1936 - 2015)
Appreciation for upholding and persevering our Ancestral Traditions and selflessly sharing to elucidate the world.
Rest In Power

Table Of Contents

Chapter 1
African spiritual universe and cosmology   1
Nature of Existence   1
Order and Balance   2
The interconnectedness of things   3
Social & Spiritual Hierarchy   4
Cyclical existence   5
Spirit of being   6
African conceptions of the Creator/'God'   7
The Creator/ 'God' as Nature   8
The creator/God as female   10
As Male and Female pair   12
As Spirit Energy & Consciousness   13
As Ancestor   18

Chapter 2
Nature and its Forces   22
The Natural Forces   24
As Agents of Social & Personal Development   30

Chapter 3
Nature of Humanity & Purpose   37
As a Spirit Being   39
Destiny or Divine Purpose   41
Dreams   44
Divination   45

Chapter 4
The Ancestors   49
Ancestors   51
Deified Ancestors   52
Communicating with Ancestors   53

Chapter 5
African forms of Veneration 59
Prayers 59
Shrines & Altars 60
Sacrifices 62
Libation 64
Offerings 65
Singing 65
Dancing 66
Drumming 68
Meditation & Yoga 69

Chapter 6
Rituals For Living 73
Communal rituals 74
Individual rituals 76
Aspects of a ritual 77
'Witchcraft'/'Sorcery' 82

Chapter 7
Recognition & Respect 89

Foreword

Despite the interest that people of African heritage have in the spiritual realm there are surprisingly few books that have so far been written that give an overview of the indigenous African spiritual heritage and its dispersal to the African Diaspora. This book, Ancestral Voices: Spirit is Eternal, is one of those few exceptions. At once scholarly but very simply written, this book deserves a place in every home.

Scholars and teachers have written and taught learnedly on Africa and religion including Professor John Jackson, Professor Yosef ben-Jochannan, Professor Charles Finch and Ashra Kwesi. However their works largely demonstrated the African influence on the Abrahamic religions.

They did not discuss the African heritage itself in any particular detail. Other writers presented detailed accounts of the spiritual systems of their own locality in Africa but they did not attempt to connect and synthesise their knowledge with the other African spiritual systems to tell any big narrative. Professor John Mbiti was the exception.

He attempted to join the dots and presents African spiritual systems in a comprehensive and coherent way. Consequently he dominated the scholarly arena on the African spiritual heritage from 1969 until now. His **African Religions and Philosophy** is a classic.

This new book, Ancestral Voices: Spirit is Eternal, is therefore a welcome addition to the field. It builds upon the skeleton created by Professor Mbiti but adds much meat onto that skeleton. The author draws upon and synthesises more recent research that was then unavailable to Professor Mbiti.

Moreover, the book includes some of the traditional spiritual systems practised in the African Diaspora. Again, this is a welcome advance on Mbiti.

Ancestral Voices: Spirit is Eternal provides a practical and relevant understanding of African spiritual systems showing their commonalities in ideas and practices from all over Africa and its Diaspora.

The author details the richness and the sophistication of the spiritual systems proving that they are in no way inferior to the Abrahamic and the other spiritual systems.

The book also provides the relevant details to show the differences between the different spiritual systems.

The author is careful not to present these different systems as a homogenised whole.

The book thus provides an excellent starting point for people who want to engage with and embrace this ancient heritage.

This is a particularly crucial issue since more and more people are seeing the holes in the Abrahamic religious heritage and wish to go deeper.

In writing the book, the author confronts the racist and religious bigotry that unfortunately still dominates the discourse surrounding African spiritual systems.

Despite living in a so-called Secularised Age, misinformation dating from the colonial era and their missionary agents still dominate the field.

This misinformation is the biggest single reason why so many Black people today are ashamed of their African spiritual heritage.

This book could not have come at a more opportune time. As most of the West is becoming more and more secular with an anything goes mentality, Christian Zionism is dominating Christianity in America on one hand and by right wing anti-government Second Amendment Christianity on the other.

Elsewhere, Wahhabi Islam is on the rise and spreading like wildfire. These hard line religious traditions are influencing Black people all over the world, especially those who have not done their own due diligence.
The big question we should be asking in this confused and conflicted era is: what are the African spiritual systems about? What are they saying? This book answers these questions.

Robin Walker

CHAPTER 1

African spiritual universe and cosmology

In beginning our exploration of African spiritual systems, it is necessary first to outline some key concepts and ideas that are important if the reader is to arrive at an accurate understanding of the contents of this book.

Especially when we discuss the nature of the African Creator, humanity, ancestors and particularly, ritual practices for veneration and manifestation.

It is necessary because these systems go beyond what we commonly understand by the word 'religion' as the impact of the spiritual philosophies of Africans extends beyond dogma and prescribed days for commemorations and veneration.

It is expansively much more and has "shaped their cultures, their social life, their political organisations and economic activities."[1] (Mbiti, pg10).

This introductory volume of work will focus on those areas that will aid the reader in attaining a body of knowledge that will be useful in cultivating a spiritually informed and enriched life experience. These fundamental concepts that inform the philosophies and practices include:

Nature of Existence

In the African worldview, the nature of existence does not comprise solely of what we can perceive with our visual sense, that is, our eyes.

The Universe is composed of two aspects or realms- the physical and spiritual realms - with the spiritual realm further stratified into various spaces or abodes.

These spaces include those of departed ancestors, spirits (deities) and that of the penultimate source of creation of all things in existence. These two realms are in constant interchange with each other and what happens in one realm can have an impact on the other. In so doing, order and harmony are maintained in the cosmos and on earth.

In fact, in some communities such as the Dagara (Burkina Faso) and Akan (Ghana) of West Africa and Vodun adherents in Haiti in the Caribbean, it is held that when we sleep our spirits journey via dreams into this invisible realm to enact causes that have corresponding effects in the physical realm.

It is also the reason why in continental African and Diasporic communities, dreams are highly regarded as containers of useful information that can aid in manoeuvring the physical reality we call life.

Order and Balance
Opposing but complimentary forces maintain order and balance as a necessity for harmony between realms of existence.
There can be no 'good' without 'bad', and the 'bad' is not to be dispelled entirely per say, but rather managed and utilised as a source of learning to inform future actions and attitudes.

All 'bad' things come with lessons for learning and growth, as does the 'good', and in overlooking their reasons for being in our lives, the consequent results are disharmony and disorder in the lived experience.

As such there is always a dichotomy of being with regards to all things in the African worldview and ritual is the tool used to address imbalances as well to maintain ideal states of being.

The interconnectedness of things
All things in existence have an impact on each other, and this interconnectedness and interplay is a constant dynamic. There are cause and effect relationships to be found in all experiences, acts and thoughts, and as such what we will in the mind is manifested in the flesh.

What is known in the mainstream as 'the law of attraction' also happens to be one of seven ancient universal laws identified by the Africans who inhabited the Nile Valley in ancient times, in the area now known as Egypt.

By the same token, it is understood that it is the kinetic energy expended in carrying out ritual practices that also aids in the physical realisation of the ends sought.
This theory thus provides us with an indication as to how and why seemingly unrelated acts of veneration can lead to a manifestation of the desired end goal, or aid in the maintenance of balance and harmony between individuals, communities and the cosmos at large.

This notion of interconnectedness is best summed up in the Akan proverb "Obiakofo na okum sono, nam amanson nhina di -It takes a man to kill an elephant, but the universe consumes it."[2] (Danquah, 1968: 189)

Likewise, it is also evident in the Bantu concept of Ubuntu; that each member of a collective has a bearing on others within it, and the wellbeing or otherwise of the whole is not separate from that of the individual or their immediate environment.

In Chaos Theory, 'The Butterfly Effect' would only be coined as a term describing the same concept in western science in 1961 by Edward Lorenz and espouses the same idea of the interconnectivity of events and between things.
Such correlations between empirical science and African sacred concepts remind us of a need to re-investigate African Spirituality from an unbiased and objective perspective for useful knowledge that can inform contemporary social organisation and education.

Social & Spiritual Hierarchy
It is held that the structure of the social organisation is a reflection of the same hierarchical organisation in the spiritual realm. The king is thus, the symbolic representation of the Creator/'God' and the officials in court are the various spirits (of nature, cosmic, universal) that act as the 'intermediaries' who officiate matters between the masses and king, whilst upholding particular responsibilities according to the duties of their office or powers imbued.

So for example whilst there is an official responsible for overseeing crop growth, another for maintaining discipline within the standing army and so on, in a similar manner there are different deities with various abilities or powers; for healing, agricultural work, fishing and the like.
Such differentiations further explain why it is these deities that commonly have shrines and temples dedicated to them and are usually the subject of prayers and rituals of veneration, rather than a direct appeal to the Creator/'God'.

A direct appeal to a senior figure would be considered disrespectful in social circles. Thus the same is expected in spiritual circles- one must first approach the intermediary to pass the message on.

It is this lack of understanding concerning these norms and etiquette that likely led to early European missionaries mistakenly asserting that Africans lack a Supreme Being/'God' in their cosmology and instead only worship spirits; a misunderstanding that still plagues traditional African spiritual adherents today.

Cyclical existence
All that is in creation is never lost, even when it decays, withers away and is no longer discernible by our visible senses. Instead, it is transformed into another form or function such that existence continuously replenishes itself.

This understanding explains why reincarnation is an accepted fact in African and Diasporic traditions because a person that has left the physical realm can be reborn as their spirit is ever present in the wider cosmos.
"Africans believe in reincarnation, but the African idea is not based on a written text; it is based on the belief that human beings live in a cycle, that things go around and come around. African reincarnation is based on the religion of ancient Egypt, where the priests said that we shall come back millions andmillions of times."[3] (Asante & Mazama, vol 1, Introduction.)

The notion is that one is provided with as many opportunities as necessary until they can attain their divine purpose for the benefit of self and all.

It therefore attributes to the African Creator, the ideas of justice, consideration and unconditional love without absolute judgement and condemnation. This is also why the notions of sin and hell are absent from the spiritual conceptions.

Spirit of being
In the African worldview, all things in creation have the quintessential essence (spirit) of the Creator contained within it, whether animate or inanimate; an extension of the aforementioned notion of the 'interconnectedness of things'.

This is why we find some rocks or other natural formations deemed worthy of veneration in African communities; because it as a sign of respect towards that aspect (spirit) of the Supreme Being within it. Therefore communication with the Creator can be virtually through all things.

The human body is a holding vessel for the spirit (and consciousness) of the Creator, and the ultimate aim is to seek reunification with it, which is achieved by living an exemplary life that affords one the status of 'Ancestor' upon death.

This animating essence is known by various names across Africa, such as 'Chi' amongst the Igbos of West Africa and 'Mana' amongst the Bantu of East and Central Africa.
It is also identified as the breath of life given to humans by the Supreme, as found amongst the Nuer of Sudan and the Konso of Ethiopia.

African conceptions of the Creator/'God'

The anthropomorphic conceptions of the Creator/'God' amongst Africans have never been solely confined to the human form, hence it is quite common to have more than the one title of reference with varying meanings within the same community of people that each encapsulates an aspect or function of this Divine source.
The many titles of reference given and their meanings reflect the broad approaches utilised by Africans in conceptualising the penultimate source of all things.

So, for instance, the name might mean 'the provider'- indicating the community's understanding that all sustenance comes from this source, or it can mean 'the all-powerful rock', a reference to the Creator being a source of strength/support for adherents and so on.
The Kikuyu (Kenya, East Africa) name for the Supreme, 'Ngai', means Creator, a reference to a function, whereas 'Akongo' means 'the beginner and the unending Almighty and inexplicable' for the Ngombe of Congo (Central Africa), a reference to the power and greatness of this source.
The various titles show quite clearly that Africans sought not to personalise the concept of 'God' into a human being,
"it does not make God in its image but tries to see itself in God's image. So if God is every and all things at once and we the human being, the bumblebee, the butterfly, the grass, the tree, the calaloo, the corn, we are all different expressions of that singular essence having our peculiar experiences, which all interdependent on one another for survival."[4]
(Small, 2013)

Mainstream religious attributions of God such as being Omnipotent (all powerful), Omnipresent (everywhere at every time) and Omniscient (all knowing) are also explicit in these African references to their Creator.

The Creator/ 'God' as Nature
Sobonfu Some (2013) encapsulates the importance of nature in African societies across all sectors of societies including its spiritual knowledge systems in the statement; 'In Africa, nature is everything'.
The reference to Nature is not just limited to the vegetation and soil, but also animals and the earth itself, including the four elemental sources- air, water, fire and minerals/rocks.

This by no means excludes the planetary bodies and universe at large and the constellations within it, many of which also inform particular ritual ceremonies as evident in full moon rituals or the appearance of interstellar objects such as comets or meteorites visible in the earth's atmosphere.

The Omnipresence (ever present) of Nature is evident the world over. It is all encompassing and enduring. Even where vegetation is absent or gradually erodes, it assumes the form of sand (deserts), and even in such environs, we find whole ecosystems of life forms still striving and being sustained.

The Omnipotence (all-powerful) of Nature is explicit in the destruction wrought by tsunamis, tornadoes, whirlwinds, earthquakes, fires and the like. In these 'natural disasters', we witness an awesome power that even all the technological advancements of humanity has yet to surpass or even curtail.

Its incredible power is further gleaned in its ability to sustain life in some way, shape or form even in the harshest conditions. Often its power to destroy is complementary to that of its power to create, as is observed with new growth and fertile soil after a bush fire for example- again we see reflected in this the notion of balance as covered earlier.

The Omniscience (all knowing) of nature is witnessed in the changing of seasons at prescribed times, just as the day 'knows' when to become night.
In the same vein, the planets revolve in alignment, with their phenomenal effects on earth evident for all to see- whether it's the female menstrual cycle or the tidal effects at sea and on other water bodies.
There is an innate creative intelligence that spurs on a harmonious dynamic interchange that is well beyond human comprehension.

Nature also meets many existential needs for humans. It is a source of plentiful and varied food types; plants and animals with different vitamins and nutritional qualities.
It is also a source of housing materials to meet sheltering needs, medications to help cure various ailments and so on- the list is endless regarding nature knowingly providing for our needs.

It is thus not surprising that it is conceived of as Divine and worthy of veneration across the continent and its legacy in Diasporic communities that has carried on the traditions.
It also explains why we find different formations within nature being respected as sacred.

The Masai(Kenya, East Africa) refer to Mountain Kilimanjaro as ngaje ngai, "the house of God", whilst Matabele mountain in Kuruman, South Africa is revered amongst the Zulus and Xhosa.

Trees such as the Sycamore of ancient Kemet, Baobab, Iroko and Nyame Dua in West Africa and rivers as well as vast water bodies such as Lake Bosumtwi in Ghana or Lake Bambline in Cameroun and so on.

The earth itself is also a prominent deity/spirit in the African mind and imaged as female, corresponding to the function of creating life (children) and providing for their needs (breastfeeding). Amongst the Akans (Ghana), she is revered as Asaase Yaa (Mother Earth), Ani for Igbos (Nigeria) and Maa-ndoo which means 'the wife of God', amongst the Mende (Sierra Leone) peoples (Opoku, 1978).

She is not just inanimate rocks and soil, but a living, functioning entity that can be communicated with via offerings and specific rituals to sustain a symbiotic and mutually beneficial relationship with her progeny.
The erudite Professor Charles Finch asserts that it is through observations and attributions gleaned from nature that is then extended unto 'zootypes', that is, animals, giving rise to the archetype of the 'mother goddesses'. (Walker, 2011)

The Creator / 'God' as female
The earliest depictions still on record in Africa to date are of the Creator as a female, and one with child, again pointing to the function of giving birth, that is, coming into being or form. For the ancient Africans of the Nile Valley Ta-Urt, a pregnant hippopotamus becomes a representation of the Great Mother Earth and its ability to sustain life. (Walker, 2011)

As such the feminine generative power provided the initial seed of thought, to identifying how creation came forth- as a process of birthing or becoming and therefore afforded to the female of the species. Glimpsed in this conception is the utilitarian nature of African Spirituality, such that the creator is less an anthropomorphic rendition of human beings, but rather a functional conception relating to how all things comes into being.

Professor James Small (2013) provides further evidence of this with reference to the oldest written African document from the Nile Valley- the 'Book of the Coming Forth by Day', also known as 'The Egyptian Book of the Dead'.
When the visible aspect of the Supreme Being, Ra, comes into being from his hidden and unknowable aspect, Amen and states that he came into being out of his mother Nun- the primordial waters.
Here we have another clear indication again of the feminine at the genesis of creation, with yet another reference to the birthing process as the progenitor of all life in existence.

We find the process of birthing in the cosmology of the Dogon (Mali, West Africa) as well, and even though their Supreme Creator is referenced as a 'he', Amma creates the world through four clavicles whose form are in the shape of a millet seed and very much resemble the female reproductive organs.

That they are also four in number is indicative of the four primordial elements of nature, so within the Dogon Cosmology, we find both the notions of the Supreme Being as Nature and with feminine attributes intricately interwoven together.
Notably, the Supreme Being of the Ijaw of Nigeria, 'Woyengi', is still a Mother Goddess; responsible for the creation of the universe and everything in it.

As Male and Female pair

There is more surviving recorded evidence of the Creator as a male and female pair in existence as opposed to singular male God-heads. As previously covered in the genesis story of the ancient Kemetians, the male aspect, Ra, is borne out of the female, Nun. (Small, 2013).

Amongst the Akans, it is Nyankopon Kwame (Male) and Asaase Yaa (Female), for the Fon (Benin & Nigeria) and Ewe (Togo & Ghana) peoples Mawu-Lisa embodies the dual nature of the Supreme Being and is still retained in its legacy in Haitian Vodun in the Caribbean as the two serpents; Damballah-Wedo and his 'wife' Aida-Wedo.

The conceptualisation of a dual nature to the Creator is recognition of the involvement of both a masculine and feminine principle for creation to come about.

Even the designations of the father being in the sky (above) and the mother being the earth (below) alludes to one of the seven universal principles of Ancient Kemet (Egypt)- 'As above, so below' - the principle of balance.

Even the spatial roles assigned can be imagined in the sexual position, popularly known as the 'missionary position', with the man on top and the woman beneath.

An allegory for this can be imaged in the rain falling from the sky (sperm) that then fertilises the earth (womb), leading to the consequent sprouting and development of life.

It is thus easy to understand how and why the masculine principle (male) is held in African societies to represent the 'beyond comprehension' or 'unseen' aspect of creation whereas the female is the visible and 'discerned' aspect. Also why it is often held that the 'spirit' of the child is assigned to the father whilst the blood/body is to the mother.

It is important to note that these conceptions do not carry with it the semiotic associations of power as found in western ideological frameworks such as, because the male is 'up', it is more powerful than the female who is 'down'. Instead, it is a reference to a complementary and harmonising state of affairs necessary for creation to occur.

"Therefore, the sky and the Earth, respectively, the masculine and the feminine concepts of origin, as well as the metaphor of the two halves of a calabash, are also powerful symbols of creation in the traditional African systems of beliefs and are conceived exactly as any African compound."5 (Asante & Mazama, vol 2, pg 619)

As Spirit Energy & Consciousness
Beyond the attribution of masculine and feminine principles in gendered forms, the Creator is also envisioned as a formless, self-conscious and intelligent entity. It supports the reference to the Creative Source being Omnipresent- ever present and everywhere, at all times, within all things.

As a state of energy, it is beyond form and containment and can transmute into all forms, hence the various forms manifested on this earth.
It is held that this essence, or spirit of the Creator, is what is present in all things- both animate and inanimate- and gives form and life.

In African spiritual philosophy, there are many different expressions of the Creator/God and an unlimited number of the forms it can take, hence why it is not uncommon to have Africans paying homage to a range of naturally occurring forms with no mental conflict as to its Divine nature.

It is also the basis of reverence for spirits/deities/Forces of Nature, because they are understood to reflect a particular aspect of the Supreme Being.

What are known as Orishas, Obosum, Nkisi, Neteru etc are but microcosms of the all-encompassing macrocosm- the Supreme Being -but more will be covered on that in the relevant chapter. It is also one of the reasons why we hardly find shrines dedicated to the Supreme Being in African communities or prescribed days, times and places for prayers and observances.
It can happen at anytime and anywhere, as the presence of the divine source is constant. It is also the reason why proselytising is absent in African Spirituality because if the understanding is that we are all of 'God', then how can one convert another back to 'God'? Simply by way of adhering to a set dogma?

The all-pervasive and imminent nature of 'God' from the African worldview is best summed up in the Akan proverb 'If you want to speak to God, tell it to the wind'. It does not mean to say the Supreme is the wind, but rather that it is Omnipresent and unfathomable in form or space.

Also that there are no prescriptions for times or dates for prayers and veneration; the channel for communication is always open. Therefore, human beings are Spirit Beings first and foremost, not just the bodies or physical containers housing that animating spark, which follows then that in the African conception, all in existence are but different manifestations of the Creator.

'The bee is in me, the bird is in me, the fish is in me, I am in the fish. In other words, life is one. It is wrong to separate the different faces of God because as we say in Zulu "God is one" even on the furthest ends of creation. God is one.

He or she, she is many things just as the earth is many things, the earth is the tree, the earth is the rock, the earth is water, so is God, so is the human being."[6] (Mutwa, 2013)

It is explicitly expressed in the concept of the Chi (life force) in Igbo societies, this Chi is present in all things and is also the essence of the Supreme Deity, Chuwuku.
Similarly, Ase, the manifestation principle or life force concept within the Yoruba traditions, expresses the same notion. It is contained within the life-blood of humans, animals, plants and rocks alike and as a result, the Ase of Orishas can be invoked into inanimate objects such as stones for initiates of Shango, as an example. Likewise, the Dogon also of West Africa refers to this life force as 'Nyama' and is held to be transmittable from generation to generation and is also contained within the blood stream. (Dieterlien & Griaule, 1986)

In Central, East and Southern Africa, amongst the Bantu peoples, it is known as 'Mana'(vital/life force) and is contained in everything. Higher cultivation of it is held to confer material benefits and blessings to one's life experience.
Amongst the Nuer of East Africa (Ethiopia), it is referred to as the life breath that sustains life and which returns to unite with their Creator Kwoth when one passes on.

That this spirit/essence of the Supreme is also self-aware (conscious) is evident in some African narratives of Creation where the source wills itself into being through the transmutation of thought/mind energy into physical matter.
In the ancient Kemetian texts (Book of the Coming Forth by Day) mentioned earlier by Professor James Small (2013), we find evidence of this in the dialogue concerning Ra.

He says of himself after becoming visible or taking on form from his 'hidden' self, 'I create myself out of myself. I cause existence to begin to exist when I begin to exist.
When I became conscious of myself, existence began to exist. I came from my mother Nun.'

What we are presented with are two notions; self-replication and birthing or becoming another form, as indicated by the change in 'gender'. Professor Small contends that what the discourse illustrates, in essence, is an allegory for 'Solid matter emanating out of liquid matter'.
Whereas this notion would have been treated with incredulity in Western science a few decades back, such a notion is now an accepted theory within the discipline of 'Quantum Physics'.

Dr. Kofi Bempah (2013) also states that in the creation story of the Akan, "God created a thing (Adie). Singular, a thing, not things, this is another way of saying that God willed and became. In the becoming mode, he assumed energy.
So we have wisdom (God) and Energy. Of course, matter is congealed energy so (a) human being is Matter and Divine spirit. The body is the matter and all created things disintegrates, but the divine aspect of man lives on forever, it is immortal."[7] (Bempah, 2014)

Likewise, for the Dogon, Griaule & Dieterlen (1986) inform that "Amma created his own twin, that is, the universe itself. Just as the universe is the replica of Amma and contains him, this universe was- and will remain – contained by Amma in the form of signs."[8] (pg86)
"Amma performed the work of creation in several stages. This work consisted of giving volume to that explosive force he had conferred on his own thought, projected outside of himself while

he was materializing the world...Amma produced his own creation by "opening (himself) up."[8] (pg 184)

On the use of the mind to manifest creation; "When Amma began (tono) things, he had his thought in his mind. The thought he had written (tono) in his mind.

His thought, it is the first figure (tonu) – Amma kize tonoy-go ku bonnu vomo-ne azubu vomo sebe. Azubu vomo ku bonnu vomo-ne tonu, azubu vomo tonu polo voy."[8] (pg 109)

What makes these notions particularly insightful and useful is that we find the will and creative use of the imagination as crucial elements required in the manifestation of desired outcomes in ritual practice.

The underlying principle being that the energy expended in bodily movements and the mind (thought), can manifest that which is visualised through energy transmutation, but this will be explored further in the chapter on rituals for living.

In much of contemporary popular and literary culture, self-help books such as 'The Secret' and 'Think and Grow Rich' amongst others, all espouse the principle of the 'law of visualisation' for achieving one's goals and aims.

It is recommended by athletes, psychologists and even in branches of scientific endeavour such as Neuro-Linguistic Programming (NLP).

It is presented almost like a newly fangled concept within human activity, not an ancient African principle of manifestation and creation, thus removing an important contribution to world history and civilisation.

Such actions thus only further ignorance of what African Sacred Sciences encapsulate.

As Ancestor
The understanding that the Creator's essence is imminent in all things is a contributing factor to the conception that the Supreme Being/'God', is also the very first Ancestor or progenitor of some communities.

"African cosmological and religious interpretations of the world show commonalities that conceive the spirits and even the first creator as sharing the same life experiences, needs, and attributes as those of the average human being" (Asante & Mazama, vol 2, pg 619).

The Dogon of West Africa hold this to be true of Amma; "Having thought and then designed the world he wished to create, Amma tried as an experiment to superpose a bit of every kind of substance that formed a "flesh" originating from his own person, a "dross" to which he added his saliva."
(Griaule & Dietressen, pg 100).

The Shona of Zimbabwe similarly conceive, the 'Mwari Triad- the Father, Mother and child trinity in their cosmology, to be related to their legendary king Soro-Re-Zhou.' (Asante & Mazama, 2009). For the Bakongo of Central Africa, one of the names for the Creator- Nzambi- is also interchangeable with that referring to human beings, nzambi.
The Akan have the saying 'God is the first Ancestor' and Credo Mutwa confirms that the very name of the Creator amongst the Zulus, Nkulunkulu, means 'Great Ancestor'.

It thus sheds further light as to why ancestor veneration is so important in African societies because it goes merely beyond just honouring the memory of a direct relative or seeking their assistance, it is ultimately an act of reverence to the Supreme

Creator. It is therefore not surprising that transitioned ancestors can be deified, particularly those who lived exemplary lives of benefit to the wider community and set worthy examples for emulation.

Elevating them to this sacred status, again, reflects the understanding that human beings are conceived of as aspects of the Creator having individually lived experiences, but on death, return to that source to reconcile again with it.

"However, an ordinary person could become a part of the god head if the society deified him or her if their deeds were great enough. Shango is now regarded as a Yoruba deity but was originally a Yoruba king whose contribution to metallurgy ultimately led to his deification.
In the Ancient Nile Valley, the same thing happened to Asar or Ausar. The Greek historian, Diodorus Siculus, portrayed him as a ruler in Ancient Sudan. At a later date, he was deified and became the deity of resurrection in the Nile Valley. Greek sources call him by the better-known name of Osiris."[9] (Walker, pg 14)

In the same Nile Valley, we find this to be the same for Imhotep, the world's first recorded multi-genius; builder of the Sakara pyramid and renowned physician. (Walker, 2011).

Moving further south of the Sahara and of recent memory, the same was initiated for Okomfo Anokye of the Akan confederation (Ghana, West Africa), who summoned down the gold stool that is held to contain the spirit of power and unity of the Asante nation. In the Diaspora it still continues, with the deification of Jean-Jacques Dessalines of the Haitian Revolution.

Summary

What becomes immediately apparent in exploring the numerous African conceptualisations of a Supreme Creator is that it is primarily a philosophical pursuit for meaning, order and social cohesion as the concepts are underpinned by a functional and utilitarian focus

At its core is the understanding that the Creator is all things and is not separate from that created, thus its vastness cannot be contained in a single theory or idea.
"Using the African system of understanding, the nature of being one cannot conclude that there is only one divinity. Neither can one conclude that there are many creator deities. At best, one must accept that the nature of the divinity is one, but the attributes of the one are found in the numerous manifestations as the many." (Asante & Mazama, vol 1, Introduction)

They also afford an experiential discovery of the self, others, community and the environment to create a harmonious ecology of balance, sustainability and continuity.
These conceptions bestow upon the community frameworks for living that inspires positive ideals and values of unity, inclusivity and communality, where all things are valued and respected as important and necessary constituents or aspects to the whole.

"Africans may use all the materials that their environment puts at their disposal in order to express their ideas about God. For them, everything that surrounds them exhibits a sort of transparency that allows them to communicate directly with heaven. Things and beings are not obstacles to the knowledge of God; rather they constitute signifiers and indices which reveal the divine being"[10] (Zahan , 5)

Notes

1. Mbiti, J. (1991), Introduction to African Religion; Second Edition. England: pg 10.
2. Danquah, J.B (1968), The Akan Doctrine of God; Second Edition. England: pg 189.
3. Asante, M.K & Mazama, A (2009), Encyclopedia of African Religion Vol 1. United States of America: Introduction.
4. Small, J (2013), Video interview for Ancestral Voices 2 film, New York.
5. Asante, M.K & Mazama, A (2009), Encyclopedia of African Religion Vol 2. United States of America: pp 619.
6. Mutwa, C. (2013), Video Interview for Ancestral Voices 2 film, South Africa.
7. Bempah, K (2013), Video Interview for Ancestral Voices 2 film, London.
8. Griaule, M, & Dieterlen, G. (1986), The Pale Fox, Paris: pp 86, 100, 109, 184.
9. Walker, R. (2011), Blacks and Religion: Volume One. England: pg 14.
10. Zahan, D. in Olupona, J. (2011) African Spirituality: Forms, Meanings & Expressions. United States of America.

References

Asare Opoku, K. (1978), West African Traditional Religion. Nigeria: FEP International Private Limited.

Bempah, K. (2010), Akan Traditional Religion; The Truth and the Myths. England.

Fu-Kiau, K. (1980), African Cosmology of the Bantu-Kongo. Canada.

Jahn, J. (1958), Muntu: African Culture and the Western World. West Germany.

MacGaffey, W. (1986), Religion and Society in Central Africa: The BaKongo of Lower Zaire. United States of America.

Morodenibig, N. (2011), Philosophy Podium: A Dogon Perspective- Second Edition, Illinois.

Temples, P. (1945), Bantu Philosophy. United States of America.

Chapter 2

Nature and its Forces

The deep reverence for nature within African Spirituality is derived from observations of natural phenomena.
It forms the basis for anthropomorphic, cosmological and phenomenological principles for living and knowing about the Creator or 'God'.

It is firstly perceived as the physical manifestation of the Supreme Being and contains its essence or life force, "African mystical theology affirms that the one life that God is expresses as all life forms. Each life form is a divine idea in expressive form."[1] (Lartey, 109).

This principle sheds much light on why there is always an inclusion of natural elements in ritual practices; it is a symbolic invitation for the Supreme to partake in the process as a means of ensuring a successful outcome (Beauvior, 2012).
The understanding being that the inclusion of the natural elements will provide direct access to its inherent manifestation force- Ase, Chi, Mana, etc- which will aid in creating the requested objective(s) in the physical reality.

This is why it is incorrect when those of other religious orientations claim that Africans worship the Earth, because the veneration is directed at the essence within, not the visible physical manifestation.

Secondly, Nature is understood to be but an extension of human beings, as Credo Mutwa asserts of the Zulu spiritual philosophies 'We are everything in everything. I am in the tree, just as the tree is in me. That is why our people had such a deep respect for life'[2] (Mutwa, 2013).

His assertion reaffirms the notion previously covered concerning the 'interconnectedness of things'; that whilst forms may be different, they are all interlinked as they share the same essence by virtue of originating from the singular Source.
Therefore, the deep respect for Nature is understandable because the African does not see themselves separate from Nature, but rather a part of it.

The physical evidence for that is obvious in the manner in which a dead body decomposes and eventually transforms into the same state as that of the Earth.
It also explains why it is a spiritual system that promotes an ecological balance between humans and their environment.

Thirdly, Nature also acts as a teacher and guide. It provides a direct medium for communicating with the Creator. It is through signs and symbols within Nature that adherents can discern relevant information and pertinent messages.

The type of animals that appear at various times within one's life, for example, may be an indication of future events yet to transpire or a sign to indicate that an offering or request has been successful. Using these guides, the practitioner is better able to interpret and understand events and situations in which they find themselves.

The multitude of expressions and phenomena within natural forms also gives rise to many archetypes or ideas about the nature of the Creative Source. The form of a mountain differs from that of a hill, as that also differs from that of a boulder and so on, yet all originate from the one source.

Lighting, thunder, storms, fires, etc all perform different functions but still aid in the continuity of life or its regeneration.

Such observations and perceptions consequently indicate to the African mind that the Creator cannot be homogenous and uni-dimensional, but rather a multifaceted, multifunctional entity with many aspects to it.

These different aspects or manifestations of the Creative Source are what is held to be the Forces within nature, also commonly referred to as divinities, deities and often incorrectly as 'demi-gods' in African Cosmology.

The Natural Forces
The Natural Forces are known by a wide variety of names in various communities but are a mainstay within the cosmological conceptions of all African communities.
The Ancient Kemetians referred to them as the Neteru (Forces of Nature), in West Africa, they are known as Orisha (Nigeria), Abosum (Ghana), Nkisi, Minkinsi amongst the Kongo, BaKongo and other Bantu peoples of East, Central and Southern Africa and so on.

In the Diaspora, in places such as Brasil and Cuba, the term Orixa is still retained with modifications in spelling to suit the current language of expression.
In Haiti, they are known as the Lwas and are often renditions of the same Yoruba Orishas as well as additional ones conceived of in the new world.
In Suriname, the Winti pantheon of the Elemental Forces are known as Tapu-Winti or Tapu Kromanti and these are also, largely derived from the Akan cosmology of ancient times.

Much misinformation was deliberately constructed around these forces within Nature to stigmatise African spiritual systems through the work of early missionaries.

They incorrectly concluded that the veneration of these forces was a confirmation that Africans did not have a supreme 'Godhead' so rather worshipped an array of 'lower gods'.

The absence of shrines or temples to the Supreme also helped to further these misconceptions, because within other religions there is always a synagogue, church or mosque held to be the 'house of God'.

Yet in the African worldview, the immensity of the Creator is too vast to be housed in a single structure, as it "exists in all things at the same time"[3]. (Small, 2013)

This misconception about the Forces also provided the basis for claims that African Spirituality was about 'idol-worship' because Africans could be seen prostrating in front of objects such as stones, carvings, masks, trees, etc. The assumption made was that it was the objects being worshipped, rather than the essence of the Force invoked into it.

Thus the foreign mind, not being able to conceive of such a phenomenon, or rather choosing to wilfully ignore it, incorrectly concluded that such objects were 'fetishes' or 'idols'.

A great many families during the colonial period would make a show of distancing themselves from their ancestral heritage by publicly burning these objects as a sign of acceptance of the newly imposed religious doctrines.

A futile and empty gesture in and of itself as such acts were mere symbolic appeasements to the new order rather than a confirmation of the 'death' of the Force per say.

These archetypes concerning the Natural Forces are not be conceived of in the same vein as the pantheon of 'gods' found in the mythological stories of other traditions, e.g., the Greco-Roman, as this only adds to the confusion about what they essentially entail.

Firstly, they are not autonomous entities separate from and functioning independently of the Supreme with their individualised powers, as found in the Greco-Roman stories.

Secondly, their usefulness is not confined to explanations about supernatural phenomena but rather, also has important functions in the development of the self; mentally and physically, as well as for social organisation.

Thirdly, they are not external to the human being, but rather exist as aspects of our being; both mentally and physically, in pretty much the same way that Nature is conceptualised as an extension of the human being.

Professor Small gives a poignant explanation of how substantial and wide-reaching the concept of the Forces of Nature are and its connection and importance to humanity; as archetypes of information explaining aspects to the human body and mind as a microcosm of the universal macrocosm.

'They are what we call in this society Laws of Physics. They are powers that exist in nature, in plants, elements and animals, in each cell and organ in the human body and the greater cosmos. They also exist as a process in each system of the human body, from the respiratory system, the lymphatic to the digestive.'[4] (Small, 2013).

So for instance, Ogun, widely referred to in the mainstream as the 'God of War', is on a deeper level of understanding a reference to the principle of transformation; from iron ore in its natural state to being made into useful tools such as cooking pots, jewellery, farming tools, etc. Iron also happens to be a vital constituent of the human blood.

Shango is exemplified in the ability of the body to conduct and generate electrical charges, similar to lightning in a thunderstorm.

As an archetype 'he' is also a reference to achieving a state of Enlightenment' or 'success'- that eureka moment when one clearly discerns the very essence of things. Hence Shango is said to 'Illuminate the Darkness', indicating a mental process of moving from ignorance to understanding and knowledge.

Yemoja and the other water divinities are the water content making up about 80% of the human body and an essential component for human survival. It sheds further light on why 'her' attributes often include notions such as nurturing and sustenance, in much the same way a mother is essential for the growth of a child and its nourishment.

"So our faith is beautiful because we exercise it in every way, even sleeping because in sleep, we dream and we have messages. The deities can catch us sleeping and gives message to move to the community, to ourselves and to the brothers. So in reality, my body is a depository of an Orixa."[5] (Figueiredo, 2014)

They are usually anthropomorphised as male or female and have a traditional priest or priestess that officiates on their behalf, prescribing the necessary rituals and customs associated with its veneration by members of the public.
They can also be animals and natural forms as well as previously discussed. "Anthropomorphism is when you use a person, an animal, a plant, a bird or fish to represent a concept, an idea or principle"[6] (Small, 2013)

Their 'powers' or essence is not restricted by geographical limitations either and there has been documented accounts of Ancient Forces summoning individuals in the Diaspora, some who have no knowledge or connections to their ancestral heritage lost over hundreds of years ago due to Trans-Atlantic enslavement, to become priests and intermediaries. (Ephirim-Donkor, 1997)

The number of forces in each community varies and is often shaped by the terrain as well. People living in a savannah will have a range different to those living in a forest or near water bodies. The environment to a large degree determines the nature and functions of the range of Forces within the spiritual cosmology.

There are also differences in the types of forces. There are those that are ancient in origin and have served communities from time immemorial and those of recent origin.
The latter tend to be solely in the possession of individual priests(tesses) and their shrine houses.
These individuals may function as the sole medium for channelling their messages or as recipients of their power in the practice of magic or healing.

This is perhaps most evident in the Diaspora where under extreme conditions of oppression and subjugation, new Forces were made manifest and added to the cosmological pantheon.
In Haiti for example, the 'new' Forces are referred to as 'Petro' spirits and similar are also found in Cuba and Brasil.
An example being the Force Agayu in the Santeria pantheon, an essence correlated with the power of the Volcano but absent in the original pantheon in Yorubaland, presumably because of the absence of volcanoes in this terrain.

They are neither 'good' nor 'bad', in African Spirituality, there is only cause and effect. The Forces only act in accordance with the wishes of the seeker, with the implicit understanding that there will be a corresponding consequence to all requests granted, as their existence is primarily to serve the living in attaining their desires and objectives.

Misuse of their power is a counter-productive endeavour in that they are held to punish those who do not use their powers for the social good but rather self-gratifying ends.

The imbalance that results from such conceited acts must ultimately be rectified for harmony to re-'attained'. In contrast, those who invoke and utilise their power(s) with integrity, honesty and for the public good are blessed with a fruitful and rewarding life.

Therefore the onus is on the individual to act in a manner that glorifies the positive aspects to the Force(s).
In light of these actions they are sometimes referred to as 'spiritual police' or 'spiritual guardians'- acting in the interest of the public good and enacting punitive measures for those who fall foul of their expectations.

They are not to be conceived solely as existing externally to the body but also as an inherent part of the human body and mind, and that latter point is one that is widely missing from discourses often had about this topic, fuelling further misunderstanding.

It must be remembered that the Natural Forces are not seen as separate to the Creator, but rather the different ways through which it manifests. So as the human body contains the life force of the Creator, so also it contains the varied aspects of it.

"The traditional African religions saw the divine power or powers as near (or immanent) and far (transcendent). The divine power or powers were held to be within all of us and dwell in all things. The divine power or powers are also out there somewhere in the Heavens."[7] (Walker, pg14)

The conception of Natural Forces within African Cosmological thought, therefore, provides much more than just a means for understanding the concept of 'God' or a Creator to our physical reality. They also provide a useful mental framework for self-understanding and development, communal organisation that seeks balance and harmony in alignment with how Nature as Creator is also observed to be functioning.

These archetypes afford a deeper mental exploration of the self, to depths of the mind where rationality and empiricism may well fall short, for discovering essential aspects of our being and our relationships with others.

Areelson, an Ogan of the terreiro Terreiro Ilê Axe Iya Nassô Oká in Bahia, Brasil, reminds us of the social and spiritual value they hold for us once we broaden our understanding of the Natural Forces through study.
"I have never doubted the Orishas, our faith is fed everyday, because as long as the practitioner is learning, becoming an adept of Kandomble, you begin to know things, your faith gets expanded, so you look right and you see an Orisha, you look left you see another one. Sometimes you are in danger needing help and an Orisha appears to help.
Even I, last May, was a victim of an assault, robbery, and while it was happening I called for Ogum and Esu, he (the thief) only managed to take a couple of my belongings, and the rest he pretended not to see when I asked the Orisha."[8] (Chagoes, 2014)

As mentioned in the first chapter, people who have lived inspirational lives and in this case particularly remarkable lives, are revered as Deified Ancestors and added to the Cosmological Pantheon over time in some communities.
Auser(Osiris), Imhotep of Ancient Egypt are such examples, Shango and Okomfo Anokye in West Africa and, the legendary king of the Shona in Zimbabwe, Soro-Re-Zhou, Jean-Jacques Dessalines of the Haitian Revolution and so on.

As Agents of Social & Personal Development
There is a range of taboos and prohibitions associated with the Forces of Nature in all African communities, Continental and Diasporic alike.
These are not simply to do with matters of ethics and morality per say, but most importantly about sacredness, consideration, respect

and value for other living things that one is in contact with on a regular basis.

Taboos vary in nature and purpose; from 'professional' ones solely for traditional priests to adhere to and others reserved for devotees of particular Forces, to dietary requirements and expected social behaviour and norms amongst others.

For instance, initiates of Orisanla are not allowed to drink palm wine. This is because, in the Yoruba story of creation, Orisanla was responsible for the creation of human and subsequently made mistakes after getting drunk leading to the formation of disabilities in humanity. The lesson behind this taboo becomes immediately clear: abuse of alcohol can have harmful consequences for self and others.

Children are warned not to collect rainwater in the hollow of the palm when it is raining else they would be struck by Shango as a punishment. Such a narrative lays bare the idea that such actions could direct the trajectory of a thunderbolt to the child and most likely lead to death. (Asante, 2009)

Similarly, in Akan tradition, children are warned not to whistle at night because it would incur the wrath of Mmotia (small dwarfish beings said to inhabit the forest) who would then come to take them away. Again we can glean the purpose of such a taboo; making noise at night will only disturb another's sleep.

Immediately the value of the allegories, taboos and narratives surrounding the archetype of the Forces becomes clear: to aid in developing useful modes of behaviour and thinking that would guide a community to learn to live in harmony and carry out its essential processes.

It is not only via taboos that we can identify the usefulness of the principles embodied within the Forces of Nature.

Their efficacy for mental development to promote effective patterns of behaviour is hardly referenced in discourses around African Spirituality, save for it being 'sheer superstition'.

"Dr Femi Biko has long taught that traditional African religions internally policed the mind. He suggests that this is a more effective way of reducing crime and building social order than the state externally policing the body"[9]
(Walker, pg 17)

The fight for freedom by enslaved Africans in Haiti from chattel slavery, following the Vodun ceremony at Bois Caiman in 1741, highlights the inherent power within these archetypes beyond taboos and expected social behaviour.
Under the mantle of Ogou (from the Yoruba Ogun), these Africans fought fearlessly armed with little more than farming tools against the most advanced military forces at the time of the French, Spanish and British and emerged victoriously.

The victory cannot be explained away simply as a 'magical' or phenomenological act alone, but also reflects the psychological motivation provided by the archetype that aided fearlessness, solidarity and an assurance of victory.

Ogun is largely known as the Yoruba 'God of War', yet it is also understood to be the Force that ensures victory and success of objectives. 'He' clears the path of all obstacles, thus it is rather telling that it was this Energy that was invoked to carry forward the liberation movement at this historical gathering of Africans in the Diaspora.
Mentally armed with this guiding principle, the Haitians rose in unity, utilise effective military strategies and social formations to eventually shake off their shackles of oppression. Hence it is key that the Forces are explored deeper for their symbolic power, rather than to hold them simply as literal anthropomorphised human characters in a Mythology.

"The Lwa, the Orisha, Nkisi, Vodun, all of the names that we call our spirits by, all of the manifestations of God, teaches us to be our own masters. Our own masters. They teach us to be self-sufficient. They teach us to be administrators and governors of our own destinies. These are basic notions that actually have extreme importance and extreme value in the 21st Century."[10] (Desir, 2013)

Studying, meditating and focussing on these archetypes with the view to better understand their symbolic value and becoming more adept at rituals designed to invoke their essence, will then result in changes in an individual's life.
We perhaps see evidence of this most clearly in rituals for appeasing fertility deities for women trying to conceive.

In some communities, a doll is fashioned (usually out of wood) for the woman to carry around with her for a period of time. The essence of the deity is said to be invoked into it as a carrier vessel and the woman is required to treat it as one would an actual child, caring for it and giving offerings to it at prescribed times, eventually aiding in the conception of a human child.

Whilst such an elaborate and prolonged ritual would once have been dismissed as mere superstitious thought or actions from a Western empirical view, what can be better appreciated now is the importance of the psychosomatic effect of this ritual on the individual. It is not only a mental endeavour but also a physical one.

As previously covered, the conception of the African Universe is that of mind and body (the immaterial and the material) with occurrences in one realm and creating effects in the other. Therefore for the African mind, this is not imagined fantasy but rather an imagined reality; that what is being deliberated on and sought within the mind ultimately comes into being.

"An nkisi is also a chosen companion, in whom all people find confidence. It is a hiding place for people's souls, to keep and compose in order to preserve life"[11] (Thompson, pg 117)

The power of the mind, even to heal and reconstitute the physical body, has now been demonstrated in many empirical Western Science experiments too- such as investigating the curative ability of the mind after subjects are administered placebo medicines. (Effect of Placebos on Parkinson Patients, 2015).

Accepted scientific programmes of self-development such a Neuro-Linguistic Programming (NLP), work on the principle(s) that 'rewiring' or changing an individual's mental outlook and thought processes with concept associations, consequently results in changes in character, personality and being.
This is largely not very different to how the conceptualisation of the Forces of Nature archetypes have been and continue to be used by African Spiritualists, yet NLP is highly regard as spearheading developments in Neuro-Science whilst similar in African Cosmology remains 'superstition', even with evidence to the contrary.

What is rather sad about these developments in Science is that they are presented as 'newly discovered' with no reference to similar found in African practices where it has clearly been used for millennia.
Equally, branches within Neuro-Science also confirm that our thoughts do more than simply helping to conceive and perceive reality, but that they are also responsible for creating changes within the body at a cellular level. (Cancer Therapy Study, 2014)

The Forces of Nature suggest a power within the mind that can be utilised for attaining objectives beyond merely decision making and reflect a deep understanding by Africans of this power inherent for eons.

It can be said that anthropomorphising the concepts has contributed to their secular misunderstanding, but perhaps that has always been its nature and purpose; to be coded language that adherents gradually come to understand as they progress in their spiritual journey, remaining forever lost to the uninitiated mind.

'Our understanding of nature and how nature works allow us to create these things we call Deities and Orishas, but these things are concepts, ideas and principles that cause certain forces in nature to animate.
Through studying our religion we see how these things animate in nature then we learn how to cause them to animate within our own self, starting with our own personality through ethical, moral training.
Then by changing your behaviour, your belief, your attitude you also then introduce these forces to the very molecular, cellular structure in the body because those things cause changes in your body as well, based on the same forces.'[14]
(Small, 2013)

Notes

1. Lartey, E.Y.A (2013), Postcolonializing God. UK: SCM Press.
2. Mutwa, C (2013), Video interview for Ancestral Voices 2 film, London.
3. Small, J (2013), Video interview for Ancestral Voices 2 film, London.
4. Small, J (2013), Video interview for Ancestral Voices 2 film, London
5. Figueiredo, A (2014), Video interview for Ancestral Voices 2 film, Brasil
6. Small, J (2013), Video interview for Ancestral Voices 2 film, London
7. Walker, R (2011), Blacks and Religion; Vol 1. UK: Reklaw Education Ltd.
8. Chagoes, A (2013), Video interview for Ancestral Voices 2 film, Brasil.
9. Walker, R (2011), Blacks and Religion; Vol 1. UK: Reklaw Education Ltd.
10. Desir, D (2013), Video interview for Ancestral Voices 2 film, New York
11. Thompson, R.F (1983), Flash of the Spirit; African & Afro-American Art & Philosophy. U.S.A: First Vintage Books Edition.
12. Effect of Placebos on Parkinson Patients, 2015. Accessed 20th April 2016: http://www.webmd.com/brain/news/20150128/study-underscores-power-of-placebo-effect#1
13. Cancer Therapy Study, 2014. Accessed 25th April 2016: http://www.learning-mind.com/meditation-changes-your-body-on-a-cellular-level-new-study-finds/
14. Small, J (2013), Video interview for Ancestral Voices 2 film, London

References

Capone, S (2010), Searching for Africa in Brazil: Power and Tradition in Candomble. U.S.A: Duke University Press.

Etefa, T (2012), Integration and Peace in East Africa. U.S.A: Palgrave Macmillan.

Greber, J (Not provided), Communication with the Spirit World of God: Its Laws and Purpose. UK: Lighting Source UK Ltd.

Okemuyiwa, L.O (2005), Ori The Supreme Divinity. Nigeria: Es-Es Communications Ventures.

Some, M.P (1994), Of Water and the Spirit. U.S.A: Penguin Group.

Chapter 3

Nature of Humanity & Purpose
The human being is held to be composed of the same elements as that of the Cosmological Universe; a combination of matter (the body)- the visible aspect, and spirit (the 'God' essence/life force)- the invisible.
As Fu-Kia contends of the Bantu-Kongo Cosmology (pg 133), "The human being (muntu, plural bantu) is both a living-energy-being (spiritual being) and a physical being (matter)."[1]

The body merely functions as the vessel through which the spirit can complete its purpose/destiny, in the physical realm. "The physical part determines his ancestry and right of inheritance whilst the spiritual part links him with God. The spiritual part, the soul, is immortal and is connected with the destiny of man."[2] (Quarcoopome, pg98)

In this sense, life is ultimately about the flow of energy or life force(s) and it impact not only on the physical matter but also other Life Forces.
The body is of less importance as the animating spark within it is what guides and directs its processes.
"For the Bantu, a person lives and moves within an ocean of waves/radiations. One is sensitive or immune to them. To be sensitive to waves is to be able to react negatively or positively to those waves/forces. But to be immune to surrounding waves/forces, is to be less reactive to them or not at all. These differences account for varying degrees in the process of knowing/learning among individuals."[3] (Fu-Kia, pg 114)

It is, therefore, the maintenance of the spirit that deserves the most attention, with the ultimate aim being its reunification with the Creative Source.
In so doing the knowledge and wisdom that spirit has accumulated over its physical lifetime adds to and expands the

'God Consciousness'. On leaving the physical vessel, a spirit that has lived an exemplary life on earth, is then revered as an Ancestor or Deified as an aspect of the 'Creator Consciousness'. Its essence (spirit) can still be communicated with by the living as death is not a final destination. It is the body that is no more, but the spirit is ever present and immortal.

Reincarnation affords the possibility of the spirit housing many different vessels over different lifetimes; from human forms to animals, plants or other vegetation.
Therefore it can be understood why the body is held in less regard than its inherent essence. It does not mean the body is totally irrelevant, but rather that it plays the role of facilitator, not the determinant, of the individual's Divine Purpose.

The Spirit/Life Force in African Cosmology is the quintessential aspect of the human being. Without it, the body is but an inanimate mass. This Life Force is not an individualised entity either but is rather an aspect of the Creator seeking an experience that can expand its consciousness further.
It also explains why, in the African mind, human beings are not seen as separate from the Creator but rather as one and the same, that is, (wo)man is 'God'.

The aspect of the Creator that manifests as a human being lives life as an act of remembering and becoming its original state through the attainment of a Divine Purpose here on Earth. There is a range of symbols, signs and tools that aid the spirit to this end.

Divination and dreams provide clues about what must be done over a lifetime and significant events to be circumvented to attain that Destiny. Nature also provides other symbols of importance for triggering the memory, such as particular animals or people that will be instrumental in this journey.

As a Spirit Being

The Spirit, Life Force or Soul within each human being is not a singular homogenous entity, but rather multifaceted and composed of various aspects, all with a clearly defined purpose that together assist in the attainment of the individual's destiny.

In this way, one can clearly discern why in African Cosmology human beings are not perceived as being different or separate from 'God'. Just as the Creator is conceptualised as being composed of many aspects, with varied functions that manifest as the Forces of Nature, so also we find the same state of affairs with the Spirit of the Human Being.

So for instance, the ancient Egyptians' conception of the Spiritual Being identified three main components- the Ba, Ka and Sahu, whereas the Yoruba have about 5, including the Emi, Ojiji, Okan, Iye and Ori, and these are given extra terms of reference based on the roles they play.
Example, the Ori is held as the ruler, guide and bearer of a person's destiny and its role in ensuring this outcome is referred to as 'Enikeji' (Idowu, pg93).

Credo Mutwa speaks of 72 different aspects to a person's Life Force or Ithongo, as it is known in Zulu Cosmology, the Akans refer to the Sunsum as well as the Hybere, the latter being the aspect of Spirit that fulfils its preordained destiny whilst the former plays a crucial role in dream communications and 'astral travelling'. For the Nuer (Ethiopia & South Sudan), it is simply referred to as the 'breath of life' and is returned to the Creator when it leaves the body. For the Bantus of Central, East and Southern Africa it is Mana.

The Life Force is activated and cultivated in a lifetime by giving offerings and through rituals and Ancestral Veneration.

Slight variations in the components of the Life Force/Spirit based on localised cultural expressions aside, what remains standard and consistent across the board is that in the African spiritual worldview, the Spirit is that immaterial complement to the material body that originates from 'God' and ultimately seeks reunification with it.
The purpose to living life is thus "to achieve inner realization of divinity and to live on the material plane as an example of this achievement."[4] (Asante, pg 628)

Through reincarnation, it is provided with as many opportunities as necessary to fulfil this purpose. Within this conception is reflected the religious notion of 'God's unconditional love for humanity.' Rather than just being given only one chance in this physical realm before being confined to an 'eternal Hell', in the African worldview, it is the very opposite.
One gets as many chances as necessary to eventually attain the required state of 'God-consciousness'.

Particular aspects of the Spirit are responsible for travelling into the spiritual realm to identify and enact effects that are useful to the physical body upon waking up.
It performs this function when one is asleep and dreaming, hence the importance of dreams in African Spirituality as conveyors of important information.

The Spirit is as effective within the spiritual domain as the body is in the physical one and their roles are complementary. There are also aspects of the Life Force that are held to linger on in the physical realm after death.

This conception underpins Ancestral communication and reverence, as this aspect of the spirit remains as a conduit through which prayers and intentions can be directed for the manifestation of intent or guidance on how to live accordingly to attain Divine Purpose.

"When the physical body dies, says a Muntu, the dual (mwela-ngindu) of that being remains within the community or out of it. The dual of the being (Mwela-ngundu), continues to act and to talk to and among the community's members as well as to the world's community, through dreams and visions, waves, radiations, and through monumental acts"[5] (Fu Kiau, pg 71)

The Spirit component to the body is forever; there is no finality to it, and it continues to traverse the cyclical nature of time with no beginning or end, just like the Creative Source from which it originates.

Destiny or Divine Purpose
The notion of a 'Divine Destiny' is another mainstay of African spiritual systems. Human beings are not just the result of random sexual acts but rather, a cosmic agreement or contract to bring forth a spirit into this world that will aid in facilitating universal balance and harmony.
Each individual comes imbued, via his or her Life Force, with the necessary skills and talents to carry out particular deeds required of the time, useful for the family and community.

In the Dagara (Burkina Faso, West Africa) conception, these attributes are referred to as that individual's 'medicine'.
"From the Dagara perspective, this world that we know as Earth is a laboratory for many different medicines that various people are bringing and in order for us to come to this world.
A call must come from this world to the spirit world requiring of our gifts. And when the call comes, and we see that it fits the kind of gift we can offer to this world, we then respond back by saying yes and hence our journey from the spirit world starts.
This journey requires of us to put specific people in our lives to remind us at critical times why we are here.

So as we journey from the spirit world to this one, there is a convergence of other spirits who also journey to support us to achieve our purpose ... so our mission here is first to test out the medicine that the SOS was sent out for us to bring."[6] (Sobonfu, 2013)

It is widely acknowledged that this Destiny or Purpose is one that is mutually agreed with the Creator before one is born and the point of living thus becomes the attainment of this objective. Even though it carries with it the notion of 'Predestination', there is no certainty that it will be attained in a lifetime nor is it set in stone so to speak.

The trials and tribulations that one will face across a life journey may result in the individual not fulfilling its requirements; therefore it is given the opportunity to reincarnate to try again and again, as often as may be necessary.

Beyond providing an existential reason for being, it is also a sacred notion that lays the blueprint for one to recognise and discover their inherent Divinity.
It places the onus on the individual to be as reflective and introspective as possible regarding thoughts, emotions and actions, for the realisation of one's true essence.

It is only by truly discerning the inner workings that one fully understands one's potential and the complete self, as reflected in the Ancient Kemetian adage 'Know Thyself'.
Malidoma Some, Dagara initiate (Burkina Faso), also expresses this process of becoming as the finding of one's 'centre' during a lifetime. It is a process of discovery, unearthing through a deep reflection of the self and capabilities.
The aim being to gain a full understanding of what is lacking or preventing one to align with the 'God consciousness' and exemplify it in how one lives.

Ba Fu-Kia notes the same of the Bantu-Kongo Cosmology, the guidelines for elevating the mind to this state of 'heavenly consciousness' is only attained via total familiarisation with self. "As such, one has to discover, or rediscover, this walk towards the 7th direction, not only for the sake of health and self-healing, but because it empowers one for self-knowing as well. It allows us to truly become "thinking-acting-beings" [kadi-biyindulanga-mu-vanga], i.e., doers [vangi] because we are masters [nganga] to ourselves."[7] (Fu Kia, pg135)

The main pre-requisite for attaining the Divine purpose is how we treat and behave towards others. Dr Bempah says of the Akan tradition, "The way our ancestors delineated for us to follow in achieving unity with God is Yeyiye, that is beneficence, in other words, selfless service to others … look at the tree, it provides seeds and fruits, does it take part of the fruit? No. It gives it away. Look at the Sun, it gives warmth, light what does it get in return? Nothing. Take the cow, it produces milk but does it drink the milk? No, it gives it to others. That is Nature at work and that is how our ancestors have told us to imitate God and do selfless service."[8] (Bempah, 2014)

Ultimately then the notion of the Divine Destiny is about self-discovery, it is about "understanding what the nature of our power is"[9] (Desir, 2013) and for it to be realised, one has to be an active participant in its discovery.
Staying aware mentally and being open to and recognising the messages and symbols presented during a lifetime, is key to learning and remembering what must be done and how to do it.

Useful aids towards this process of remembrance are dreams and divination systems; containers of valuable information to guide and direct one towards their purpose.

Dreams

Dreams in the African conception are not merely aspects of our unconscious replaying various parts of information garnered by the conscious mind over the course of a day or a lifetime. Rather, it is often a reflection of messages and experiences of the Spiritual Being within the spiritual realm.

'They are coded messages from contact with spirit that we need to find context for, not only for the past but also the present and the future. Things overlooked in the past, those we have not been paying attention to in the present or things that may yet manifest themselves in the future'[10] (Some, 2013)

What is most important then is identifying the symbols and signs within the dream to decode the messages being conveyed and its relevance to the dreamer. Therefore it is encouraged that dreams are shared with others and elders in the family or community for further clarity and advice.

The messages contained within them are essential guidance for the living as it helps to direct them along their path of destiny and to know how to act or respond to a life situation. This is particularly critical, as there are different types of dreams too- those that speak to an individual reality and those that speak to a collective one.

Making this differentiation with regards to the type of dream helps to identify its wider significance. This is why decoding it with the help of others, as a collective endeavour, is favoured, because the extra minds can recognise symbolisms the individual may overlook or fail to understand.

It is also held that dreams constitute an actual realm of existence, where the spiritual self can journey to and perform necessary rites to achieve harmony and balance in the physical world.

In the New Age movement, this is popularly referred to as 'Astral Travelling'.

As mentioned earlier, it is also a realm where other spirits are active- from departed ancestors and members of the community to other Forces, be they Natural Forces or Cosmic. Within this space, a dialogue takes place where necessary information is shared with the Spirit of the dreamer.

On awakening, the dreamer is left with particular impressions in the mind that hold the keys to what must be done to avoid impending catastrophe, illnesses or conduct rites that have been neglected and so on.
The dream is much like a counselling session where one is provided with advice and information. It is a space where one is further supported along one's life journey.

In this realm, the ancestors and other forces are directly available to assist with the resolution of any issues at hand, and it is between this dialogue of Forces that one arrives at a solution and course of action to be enacted when one wakes.

"It is your subconscious mind taking the elements that was ingested by your conscious mind and having a dialogue with your ancestral mind. That's dreaming."[11] (Small, 2013)

Divination
Divination refers to the process used in foretelling one's future or identifying relevant issues yet to occur, or are occurring in one's life. It is used as a means of understanding why said events are happening and how to tackle them.

It identifies causalities and prescribes a course of action for overcoming them, usually via a ritual designed to protect one from any adverse effects or to ensure that 'blessings' expected are received without interruption.

Divinations can be performed for a range of issues; from identifying the source(s) of illnesses to determining what decision is to be made regarding an issue at hand, or even what messages ancestors may be sending from the spiritual realm, amongst others. In essence, Divination is a tool for guidance with regards to how one is to live their life and what is to be done at a particular stage in the life process.

There are many forms of divination across African communities worldwide but all with the same objectives: uncovering important information that is yet to happen or has already happened and its possible impact on one's life.

The range of materials in use also varies: Amongst the Zulus, there is the use of bones and stones amongst others, the Dogon use markings in the sand said to be in alignment with cosmic bodies.
Some Akans (Ghana) use a process of staring into water to discern events or the use of 'magic mirrors' to 'see', same as in parts of the Congo. In the Yoruba Ifa system (Nigeria), there is a wooden board (Opon Ifa) on which is placed wood shavings from a termite's mound, on which particular markings are made after each throw of a necklace that forms an 'Odu'.
The Odu is underpinned by a story (Odu Ifa) that reflects the situation at hand and also provides the necessary 'appeasement' that must be conducted to resolve the situation. We find similar in the Afa system of the Igbos (Nigeria) and the Ewes (Ghana) concerning the throwing of the diviner's necklace (Odigba Ifa) to discern into the reality of situations.

The markings made in the Ifa divination are binary in nature, similar to those found in the I-Ching divination system of the Chinese with Yin and Yang lines. Ifa, on the other hand, is a lot wider in scope- from the types of foods one is allowed to eat, to the kind of colours one is permitted to wear.
It represents the first use of binary data in human history.

There is also the use of Coconuts, Kola nuts and Cowrie shells amongst others. The Bwiti of Gabon West Africa can even use a person's vomit to identify issues of spiritual relevance based on patterns that can be deciphered in it.

A trained shaman usually has to undergo years of training to master the craft of performing divinations. Babalawos of the Ifa system have to train a minimum of some 30 to 40 years to be considered an adept at his craft.

It is not a random process of interpretation, as the diviner has a wide range of stimuli to draw from in the reading. The way one smells, their date or day of birth, name or parent's names, etc are all usual stimuli that can provide 'data' for 'reading'. The diviner only 'reads' what is already present in or around the person, and through contact with a person's Life Force; the diviner can discern the relevant information at the time.
So the individual is as important as the diviner, as they provide the source of inspiration so to speak.

There are also personal divinations that can be done- usually with four cowrie shells or four parts of a split coconut thrown to the ground.
Personal divinations are useful for seeking answers to questions one may be pondering that requires either a yes or no answer. When at least 2 or more fall facing upwards, this indicates a yes and any less, a no.
For more substantial questions, a trained shaman must be sought for assistance with uncovering the message at hand.

Divination in this sense is akin to a road sign that guides travellers to their chosen destination. They afford us the opportunity to look ahead and prepare for eventualities, or to seek an alternate path to travel if we are to arrive at our chosen destination.

Notes

1. Fu-Kiau, K.K.B (1980), African Cosmology of the Bantu-Kongo: Principles of Life & Living. Canada: Athellia Henrietta Press. Pg133

2. Quarcoopome, T.N.O (1987), West African Traditional Religion. Nigeria: African Universities Press. Pg98

3. Fu-Kiau, K.K.B (1980), African Cosmology of the Bantu-Kongo: Principles of Life & Living. Canada: Athellia Henrietta Press. Pg114

4. Asante, M.K & Mazama, A (2009), Encyclopedia of African Religion; Vol 2. U.S.A: Sage Publications. Pg628

5. Fu-Kiau, K.K.B (1980), African Cosmology of the Bantu-Kongo: Principles of Life & Living. Canada: Athellia Henrietta Press. Pg71

6. Some, S (2014), Video interview for Ancestral Voices 2 film, London

7. Fu-Kiau, K.K.B (1980), African Cosmology of the Bantu-Kongo: Principles of Life & Living. Canada: Athellia Henrietta Press. Pg135

8. Bempah, K (2014) Video interview for Ancestral Voices 2 film, London.

9. Desir, D (2013) Video interview for Ancestral Voices 2 film, New York.

10. Some, S (2014), Video interview for Ancestral Voices 2 film, London

11. Small, J (2013), Video interview for Ancestral Voices 2 film, New York.

References

Gonzalez-Wippler, M (1989), Santeria The Religion. U.S.A: Llewellyn Worldwide.

Knappert, J (1990), The Aquarian Guide to African Mythology. England: Thorsons Publishing Group.

Mason, J (2003), Who's Knocking on my Floor?: Esu Arts in the Americas. Yoruba Theological Archministry.

Mutwa, V.C (1996), Zulu Shaman: Dreams, Prophecies and Mysteries. U.S.A: Lakebook Manufacturing Inc.

Umeh, J.A (1999), After God is Dibia; Vol 1. Britain: Karnak House.

Umeh, J.A (1999), After God is Dibia; Vol 2. Britain: Karnak House.

Chapter 4

The Ancestors
Ancestral Veneration is the one aspect of African Spirituality that most not in the traditions are familiar with, so much so it is often the synonym used in reference to it, under labels such as 'Ancestor Worship' or 'The Cult of the Ancestors'.
Yet such phrases are colonial in origin and reflect either a genuine misunderstanding or a deliberate attempt to misrepresent it.

The role of Ancestors is indeed very prominent and understandably so. In the African conception as previously covered, there is no end to life, as such the spirits or souls of the departed are known to be still present, although in a different form. The roles that they held in the family and societal affairs are still duties they can enforce even though they have moved on to a state of spiritual existence.
"The ancestors are still not separated from their earthly families by death and therefore are still considered part of their human families. Indeed in the African context, the family is made up of the dead, the living and the generation yet unborn."[1]
(Quarcoopome, pg 128)

The status of Ancestor is not one achieved automatically by death. There are conditions to be first fulfilled. The individual would have lived a long and dutiful life; to their families and the society at large. This individual is held to be an enlightened being, one that has achieved self-realisation, as reflected in the title given them by the Akan- Nana.

"The Akans hold the state of Nanahood as the goal and fulfilment of human life…The phrase 'Nananom Nsamanfuo' meaning 'The Giver and Source of Enlightenment' is the invocation used when any Akan prays at any time to the Supreme Deity."[2]
(Bempah, pg 114)

Ancestors tend to be elders in the community as with old age comes wisdom, gathered over years of living and experience. Those who die young will not attain such a status and neither those who die in less than favourable circumstances such as car accidents, diseases such as leprosy, epilepsy or suicide, as these are taken as markers of a 'corruption' of the spirit that had manifested physically on the body.

The state of 'Ancestorhood' reflects one of 'perfection', the highest ideal state of being and fulfilment of human life. Therefore such 'imperfections' run contrary to it and are taken as an indication that the individual is not fit of such a status after death.
In some communities, e.g. the Yoruba, to die childless will also result in not being acknowledged as an Ancestor. The reason for this being clear, as there is no one left to carry forth one's lineage or remember and commemorate your existence.

Death through violence is another barrier to becoming an Ancestor, with the exemption for those who die on a battlefield, in defence of the community.
Such circumstances rather exalt the individual to the degree they may even be Deified, thus joining the pantheon of the Divinities.

The guarantee for being welcomed into the ranks of the Ancestors depends on the character one cultivates in life, the assistance they provide to others in need, how fair and equitably they conduct themselves as well as their achievements over their lifetime.

"The ancestors, having lived, died, and been resurrected and vindicated, have achieved something that no human being has- immortality. They have reached the highest state of existence comparable to God, though not God, because they cannot create or alter the created order. However, they have achieved eternal existence after first achieving perfection as elders."[3]
(Ephirim-Donkor, pg 140)

There is also a clear distinction in types of Ancestors if you will. There are those primarily venerated by family members and those whose exemplary works stretch across a community. The latter tend to be vaulted into the ranks of the Divinities. Therefore the difference in ranking it would seem, is due to degrees of influence.

Ancestors
These, in general, are those family members of old age and wisdom as covered earlier. They are the heroes and heroines who have maintained and cared for their family lineages whilst alive. In death, they are remembered and praised. Respected for their support and assistance whilst alive, the same is expected of them in death too.

The living performs their obligations in keeping their memories alive through offerings and remembrance ceremonies or rituals. In so doing, they give of their energy to the spirits of their Ancestors, adding to their Vital Force and making them 'stronger' in the spiritual realm.

It is done to ensure they are still useful to the family's needs and continues the role(s) held whilst alive. They are understood to be closer to God by being in the spiritual realm and as such can intercede on behalf of family members- as intermediaries between the Creator and humanity, to ensure the fulfilment of prayer requests and the like.

As the African Spiritual universe is a reciprocating one, the veneration performed by the living on behalf of the departed is likewise returned in favour by the departed, for the living in their times of need.
"The dead do not sever their links with their kinsmen but continue to be members of their individual families, fulfilling their obligations as elders.

Thus, they are considered active members of the families. The relationship between the dead and the living is symbiotic as each group has a part to play for mutual benefit."[4] (Asare, pg 37)

Deified Ancestors
These are those individuals whose works have benefitted the community as a whole, beyond just the family. Practically national heroes and heroines who have, through their exemplary works, left behind a legacy that has impacted all within a community.
Often they are instrumental in the founding of the communities or were successful in conflicts that threatened the whole community. In other cases too they performed legendary acts whilst alive that live on in folklore thereafter or were highly skilled in their craft.

They do not just become Ancestors per say but are also afforded the recognition as one who has indeed become like the Creator, attending to the needs of all and sundry, even those they may not be familiar with.
It is this disposition that informs their 'God'-like status, as their acts are viewed in line with how Nature provides for human beings in general without preferences given for particular individuals. It is a sacred practice amongst Africans worldwide and consistently found amongst all communities too.
Osiris was deified into the Egyptian pantheon as one held to be responsible for the introduction of wheat cultivation, as was Imhotep, the multi-skilled physician and architect, for his legendary healing and architectural skills.
For founding fathers there is Soro-Re-Zhou of Zimbabwe, Nyikang of the Shiluk and Tsoedi the first king of the Nupe.
For their spiritual prowess, there is Khambageu of the Sonjo, Okomfu Anokye of the Akans and Tampa Vita of the Congo- burnt at the stake for her role in the resistance of her community to European Imperialism.

Also Simon Kimbangu, a renowned healer, responsible for the formation of the Kimbaguist movement in the Congo. There is also Jean-Jacques Dessalines, added to the Vodun pantheon of Lwa after his transitioning, for his role in leading the Haitian nation after independence from France.

Communicating with Ancestors
As beings with the legs in both worlds so to speak, they can aid the passing on of requests, to be acted on in the spiritual world. They can be communicated with via a variety of means- altars and shrines are set up in their honour at which is offered food, drink and their favourite objects whilst alive.

"The Jengili is an ancestral altar marked out with a circle of stones, but offerings or sacrifices in it are directed to the mother of the ego or the mother of the paternal ancestors…Its function is to serve as an energetic navel on every individual and, at the same time, as an umbilical cord through which the energies flow from material and non-material forms. It is generally the place where the individual's destinies are expressed in their energetic form, transcending space and time."[5] (Morodenibig, pp 260-263)

Libation is another sacred act used to communicate with and solicit their assistance. It involves pouring water or alcohol onto the ground whilst reciting prayers for their well-being as well as any requests to be made of them.

In Ancient Egypt also we find evidence of individuals writing letters to departed ones seeking their assistance and even spaces being left unoccupied at the dinner area for them to join in with the rest of the family.
Placing a container filled with water out at night in a compound so any Ancestors or Beings that visit can quench their thirst is another common practice we find for appeasing the Ancestors and their needs.

All these symbolic acts of reverence are primarily to indicate to the departed that they are only absent in body and that the relationship continues. They are ever present, eternal and a welcomed addition to the family always.

"The African family, therefore, has a supernatural dimension to it, for it is made up of the living and the dead, both of whom have specific roles to play in the maintenance of the family and the society in general."[6] (Asare, pg 38)

There are also a range of Ancestral communal rites that are performed to celebrate their lives, in commemoration of their memories and in appreciation of their assistance that continues. Such occasions also help with social cohesion and unity within the communities.

Some examples include the Adae festivals of the Asantes, the Mendes of Sierra Leone, the Fon of Dahomey and the Mmo society of the Igbos. Masks often feature prominently in such public ceremonies as evident in the Egungun masquerades of the Yoruba and Teke or Bateke peoples of the Congo and Gabon as well as the Dogon in Mali.

The same level of respect and veneration is found in the Diaspora as well. In places such as the Caribbean and Americas, the Ancestors of the enslaved who had passed on were added to the pantheon of Divinities. Not only just the African but the indigenous Indian communities that lived in those lands before the arrival of Europeans as well from other groups such as the East Indian and Chinese.

So for example in Brasil, the African ancestors are known as Pretos Velhos whereas their Indian counterparts are referred to as Caboclos. We see similar in the Winti pantheon of Suriname and Guyanese Komfa as well.

The Ancestors also respond to the living by sending messages in dreams, through other individuals and even signs and symbols in

Nature such as plants, animals, stones and the like. Staying aware and being open to them is the only way to discern and decipher these messages.

They continually send the messages in using various forms until such time when the individual finally realises it.

"In Vodun philosophy, communication with the Ancestors comes first of all by the will of the Ancestor. On our side, we have to make a lot of effort to develop our ability and observe so when they do something to attract our attention we can notice it."[7] (Bello, 2013)

Lest we forget, the Ancestors are an internal part of us from birth; their genes exist within our DNA as we are the product of their unions over time. Ancestral communication thus reflects the attempt to activate their essence within us to draw and learn from the experience and wisdom garnered over their lifetimes, by tapping into the 'chromosome memory' inherent (Beauvoir, 2013).

Advances in Modern Science now confirm that various genetic markers in our chromosomes transmit traits, phobias and behavioural patterns between family members over generations, confirmation of this principle that Africans have been aware of for millennia without the use of high-tech laboratory equipment in use today. (Emory University School of Medicine, 2013)

It can be argued that there is a thin line between veneration and worship and if indeed, there is a difference, yet in the African mind there clearly is.

What fuels this debate of 'ancestor worship' by non-adherents of the traditions is likely because similar processes of veneration, such as offerings and sacrifices, are used for venerating both the manifestations of the Creator and Ancestors.

As such it can seem there is no difference, but in the African mind it is very clear that the veneration for the Ancestors is for recognition and appreciation, not worship.

What is most interesting is that a similar state of affairs can be observed in Western societies, the same responsible for the stigmatisation and vilification of African Spirituality over centuries. On what may appear to be on a 'secular' level, occasions such as Veteran's (US) or Armistice (UK) day and their equivalents across European countries, where war heroes are remembered for their sacrifices for the nation, are a reflection of this same notion.

These events are not altogether 'secular' either as they are often performed in conjunction with a religious institution, often churches of the various Christian denominations, so it also comes with a level of religiosity.

Likewise, the canonisation of saints, celebration of the past glories of Kings and Queens, etc or the commemoration of Avatars in Oriental religions or philosophies serve the very same purpose. The Prophets and Messiahs found in other religions are all ultimately from a family line having once lived as human beings, so they too are by default, an ancestor to someone.
It is bewildering then as to why it is sanctioned to pray to and even worship these individuals, e.g. Jesus, or Mohammed, yet it is viewed negatively when done in the context of Africans and their Ancestors.

It is, therefore, hypocritical that even in the 21st Century, Ancestral Veneration is still spoken of in the most repugnant and derogatory of terms in the mainstream by people of other religious orientations even though they perform similar, whether they are conscious or not of this fact.

Ancestral Veneration reflects or reinforces other essential elements within the African Spiritual Worldview: notions about the continuation and endless cycle of life, reincarnation and our obligation to others in ensuring their welfare- the basis for communal living.

It should be immediately clear then the value of Ancestors in African Spirituality, not as objects of worship as many try to stigmatise it with, but as role models for emulation.

"The constant reminder of the good deeds of the ancestors acts as a spur to good conduct on the part of the living; and the belief that the dead can punish those who violate traditionally sanctioned mores acts as a deterrent.
Ancestral beliefs, therefore, represent a powerful source of moral sanction for they affirm the values upon which society is based."[8] (Asare, pg 39)

Notes

1. Quarcoopome, T.N.O (1987), West African Traditional Religion. Nigeria: African Universities Press. Pg 128

2. Bempah, K (2010), Akan Traditional Religion: The Myths and the Truth. Self-published. Pg 114

3. Ephirim-Donkor, A (1997), African Spirituality: On becoming Ancestors. Eriteria: Africa World Press Inc. Pg140

4. Opoku Asare, K (1978), West African Traditional Religion. Nigeria: FEP International Private Limited. Pg37

5. Morodenibig, N.N.L (2011), Philosophy Podium: A Dogon Perspective; Second Edition. U.S.A: Firefly Productions.

6. Opoku Asare, K (1978), West African Traditional Religion. Nigeria: FEP International Private Limited. Pg38

7. Bello, B (2013), Video interview for Ancestral Voices 2 film. Haiti

8. Opoku Asare, K (1978), West African Traditional Religion. Nigeria: FEP International Private Limited. Pg39

References:

Amen, R.U.N (1990), Metu Neter; Vol 1. U.S.A: Kharmit Media Trans Visions Inc.

"Chromosome Memory" of Parental Genomes in Embryonic Hybrid Cells. By Serov, O. et al, Russian Academy of Sciences, 2002. Accessed on the 10/05/2016:
http://link.springer.com/article/10.1023%2FA:1024076808102#/page-1

Emory Universe School of Medicine research on the trans-generational transmission of traits through DNA. Accessed on the 2/02/2016:

http://www.telegraph.co.uk/news/science/science-news/10486479/Phobias-may-be-memories-passed-down-in-genes-from-ancestors.html

Fu-Kiau, K.K.B (1980), African Cosmology of the Bantu-Kongo: Principles of Life & Living. Canada: Athellia Henrietta Press.

Philosophy Podium: A Dogon Perspective (2nd edition), Neb Naba Lamoussa Morodenibig, Firefly Productios, 2011, Chicago, USA.

Tempels, P (2010), Bantu Philosophy. U.S.A: HBC Publishing.

MacGaffey, W (1986), Religion and Society in Central Africa. U.S.A: The University of Chicago Press.

Mbiti, J.S (1975), Introduction to African Religion; Second Edition. England: Heinemann Educational Publishers.

CHAPTER 5

African forms of Veneration

There are no rigid guidelines in African Spirituality for the format or forms of veneration of the Creator, or its manifestations, at an individual level. This flexibility reflects the understanding and recognition that the individualised spirit within each person can freely intuit the format of its personal relationship with the Creator, considering it is perceived as an extension of it.

'There are no dogmatic rules either for the format of a prayer, rather it is simply a talk, a means of direct communication with the unseen, with no 'formulas for success' such as 'Our Father' or 'Hail Marys' in the Vodun tradition.'[1] (Beauvoir, 2013).

As the Creator is 'in all things at once' there is no requirement for it to be performed in a particular place, day or time. It can happen anywhere, at any time, as reflected in the Akan proverb, 'If you want to speak to God, tell it to the wind'[2] (Wope Nyame aka asem akyere no a, ka kyere mframa). (Bempah, 2014)

The Creator is immediately accessible to adherents, not far removed out in the Cosmos somewhere.

Veneration can cover many uses as well, not just for requests for assistance; it can be for commemorative, celebratory and preventative purposes, amongst others.

Prayers:

In the African context, prayers involve more than just the utterance of just words or the recitation of particular phrases. African prayers also include a range of senses- use of visualisation, movement (dances or libation pouring) and scents (herbs, fire, wood bark, etc), amongst others, to heighten the experience further and engage the Life Force within.

The prayer involves first and foremost imagining the outcome(s) desired as a visual in the mind. One must envisage in as much

detail as possible and also 'experience' and incorporate any associated scents or sounds into the mental picture. Example, if one was to be praying for peace, the image could be a calm, picturesque valley as the main visual, then 'smell' the scents of the grass or flowers near the lake and 'hear' the noise of the bees and birds pollinating these plants by the lakeside.
(Credo Mutwa, 2013)
The more detail included in the mental picture, the more 'effective' the prayer is deemed to be, and the faster results will be achieved. It was mentioned earlier about the 'imagined reality' and it is in the African prayer format that we see its fullest expression.

What is interesting is that these techniques are now the stuff of many contemporary self-help discourses under the moniker 'What you visualise and believe, you can achieve'. The same methods are reportedly utilised by athletes for personal motivation and are an accepted technique within Neuro-Linguistic Programming (NLP).
Yet interestingly enough, it is accepted as factual in these areas whereas, within African Spirituality, it is still largely referred to as 'superstition'.

Shrines & Altars:
These refer to particular locations to go and focus thoughts, pray, give offerings and receive guidance and instructions in return. They provide a space within which people can focus their subconscious mind and project thoughts yet to be realised.

"An Altar or a Shrine is a material base into which a spirit can be invoked."[3] (Bempah, 2013)
They can take many forms based on the Forces contained within them as well as the uses to which they are put.

'The Shrine is a place where you harness Forces of Nature into a specific instrument or location and that's a science that only well trained high priests and priestesses can accomplish. They have the receptivity to dialogue and communicate with it to receive instructions to help those who visit the Shrine in need.'[4]
(Small, 2013)

A Shrine is a communal Altar that serves the needs of the community, rather than just the individual. It is officiated by a local shaman and can include many objects with invoked Forces that serve as guardians of the community.
It is also where collective rituals and commemorations are performed on behalf of the entire community and also where the shaman will go to receive instructions and guidance for messages to be passed on to the community and so forth.

The Altar, on the other hand, will be found in an individuals' home. It can contain objects of significance such as physical items from Ancestors who have passed on, their pictures, vessels for libation, offerings to them as well as other Forces and spirit guides. Symbolically, it serves as the doorway between worlds, where interchange takes place between the material and immaterial worlds.
Offerings and prayers are performed in front of it or by it, and likewise, messages and guidance from beyond the physical world are received in return.

' It is a place of focus, a place where you centre yourself into what you feel is most important to you. It's a guiding place reminding you of what you are and who you are. You can have things there that are part of your spiritual development because it's basically a spiritual centre. It can be dedicated to different names, people, forms, experiences and levels of development.'[5]
(Yarborough, 2013)

Sacrifices
Possibly one of the most contentious areas within African Spirituality is the offering of live animals- chickens, goats, lamb, cows and the like.
It is considered by many outside, and a few within the traditions, as an unnecessary form of animal cruelty. What those of this view are not appreciating is the most vital fact in this Cosmological worldview- Life Force.

Sacrifices are used to resolve spiritual issues and it is the Life Force in these animals that are utilised in the appeasement and resolution of these matters.
It is harnessed to 'activate' the required outcome(s) and is not an act that anyone is qualified to do. It must be done by the most highly trained shaman or only under their guidance.

In Kandomble for instance, some initiates have identified what they say are the equivalent in herbs to the sacrifice of an animal and these are used in their stead.

The Life force of the animal feeds that of the Forces to make them 'stronger' and they reciprocate with the result(s) required in the physical realm.
Animals are not forced against their will; rather a mutually consenting agreement is reached before the animal is sacrificed. There are various methods used to acknowledge this and can vary between localised systems.
"Before they are slaughtered the sacrificial animals are offered food and drink, the acceptance of which declares the animal's consent to the sacrifice. Should an animal refuse these gifts, it is led away and another put in its place."[6] (Jahn, pg 46)

Not all animals are killed using physical means such as knives, blades or other sharp instruments. Many well-versed shaman are capable of using particular, closely guarded invocations that speak to the Life Force of the animal, so it agrees to exchange its

Life Force so as to execute the deed in hand. Such high-level ceremonies are usually not a matter of the public record or viewing.

Human sacrifice is perhaps the most contentious of all, whereby a person is killed for a ritual purpose. The Asantes (Ghana) for instance, in times past, would sacrifice a human being to accompany the spirit of a deceased King as he journeys into the spiritual realm and some shaman also profess it to be the preference of their Divinities.
It has ceased over time due to governmental interventions and rather interestingly when it occurs these days, it is reportedly by people of other religious orientations who are seeking to make a quick buck.

What human sacrifice represents is, therefore, the highest form of sacrifice one can make, as the blood (Life Force) been spilt is also that of the Creator's. In doing so, the individual is seeking to utilise the most powerful and potent means to ensure they get what they seek, but at the cost of some-one else's life (taken without permission).

So on the other hand, it also represents the gravest form of perversion that can be engaged in as it contradicts the spiritual concept of Ubuntu, as well as balance and harmony in the cosmos. As to be expected, in all reported cases, those who have been found to participate in these vile acts are also meted out with the worst possible afflictions- to themselves as well as extended members of their family.

In this regard, human sacrifices fall into the category of 'witchcraft' or 'sorcery', that is, practices that are not useful for the common good nor of one's self and are viewed in a negative light and rightfully so.

Libation

Libation refers to a prayer form that involves the pouring of a copious amount of a liquid, usually water, on the ground accompanied by speech. It is a symbolic action of 'quenching the thirst' of Spirit Beings and providing them with nourishment.

In African culture, it is disrespectful to ask when one does not give, as there is no equanimity, so in line with the main tenet of balance between realms as per African cosmological philosophy, one must first give in order to receive- as above, so below. It is also a sign of respect for the ethereal beings that one is asking assistance from at hand.

It can be traced again beyond ancient Kemet and is still practised to the present day, both on the Continent and in the Diaspora. It can also be poured into a vessel or container especially if the context does not provide access directly to the earth. Libation starts with a call to the specific Ancestors and Energies to acknowledge them.

They are called by name and requested to be present to officiate the process to ensure their pleas are received favourably. The ensuing is then a talk with them regarding what is required of them.

Some libations can be accompanied by 'liturgical prayers' especially if it is a communal event and being presided over by a shaman. As these events are usually to commemorate Forces responsible for whole communities, the shaman tends to follow prescribed formats in line with traditions identified over time by his/her predecessors, as custodians of the Divinity(ies).

However, there are no such prescribed requirements for individual libations as these can be as varied in purpose as in recipients- the key is the acknowledgement and recognition of the Being(s) called in to officiate and assist.

Offerings

Offerings are pretty much in the same vein as libations- symbolic gestures of providing nourishment to the Forces- an act reflecting one's consideration and gratitude. They can take many forms too, usually based on the context.

There are offerings left at crossroads, in nature, on an altar or shrine, even in coffins for the dead and so on. There can be meat, fruits, vegetables, water, drink, sweets, cakes and even cooked meals. Offerings left in nature itself eventually becomes food for other animals in the environment so their benefit on the physical level as well is also evident.
It fosters a healthy ecological cycle and balance, with consideration and respect accorded to all beings within it.

Singing

Sound is Power, not just random noise but a potent vibrational force capable of opening the portal between realms. It carries energy as well as transfers it, so singing is another important way to aid the transference between the Spiritual and Physical Worlds.

We are aware of its power in instances where a singer's voice can be elevated to a certain pitch that is capable of cracking and shattering glass- the immaterial affecting the physical, supporting one of the keys concepts within the African Spiritual Cosmology! 'It is also known to release toxins within the body and is one of the key methods used by Africans to counter becoming depressed, as most evident in our grieving rituals and it lets life flow back into your body.'[7] (Some, 2013)

Thus we can understand why singing and other tools for creating sounds are ever present in a ritual ceremony; it is necessary to open doors and call in the Spirit Beings.

Tools such as the Asson, shakers such as the maracas or cow-bells and the like are prevalent in all systems as a harbinger of the Spirits.

For some Forces, there are specific songs of invocation that can be sung to invoke their presence. Example, there are a variety of such songs dedicated to particular Orishas, and again, these reflect the building up of 'set traditions' over time but even then, it is not proffered as 'the only way'.
Even by merely calling out and mentioning them by name is sufficient to warrant their attention and assistance. In a cosmological worldview based primarily on the interactions between energies and waves and vibrations, a call out will be understood and a response in kind will be received.

The legacy of its importance in African veneration can also be seen in the impact of 'Negro Spirituals' for enslaved Africans in the Diaspora, forcibly converted to Christianity, in enduring the sufferings they were subjected to.
"When we were brought over here (USA), we were stripped naked, we had nothing in our hands, we were beaten, burnt, separated, but we had our spirit power and that is why we survived. One thing we began to do was to sing again to one another; we never stopped singing and in that singing was the transmission of the word power, spirit coming out to one another. 'Ain't gonna let nobody turn me around', that's what we were telling one another, to never give up, that's spirit power right there!"[8] (Yarborough, 2013)"

Dancing
Dancing is not merely a 'secular' form of entertainment. As earlier mentioned, all things within the African worldview originate in spirit or is associated with it and dancing is not exempt.

Dances have a range of functions as well; from those designed to prepare the body for a smooth birthing experience to those required in rites of passage ceremonies.
There are also those specifically for communicating and interacting with the spirit world and the Beings within it. ' Dance is energised by the spirit within you'[9] (Yarborough, 2013)

As the dancer performs the necessary movements to venerate the Forces, it invokes the required energetic signature for the Spirit Being whom the dance is in reverence of, to unite with the spirit of the dancer- to use as a channel of communication to humanity. This is the phenomenon inaccurately labelled 'possession'- implying a forced state of altered consciousness.
Often those chosen to be the voice and vessel for communication do not have any recollections of what is said or done when in unison with the essence of the Divinity and specially trained assistants are on hand to translate what is conveyed to the general public.

In its amorphous form, the Forces cannot interact directly on the physical plane, thus having a vessel in human form is one such avenue available.
As such we have specific dances for particular Orishas in the Ifa, Kandomble, Lucumi and Santeria systems. Amongst the Akan the dance is known as 'Akom' literally meaning to prophesy; as the messages transmitted are often prophetic in nature.
We also find dancing into trance to bring forth spirit within the Komfa system of Guyana and Winti of Suriname in the Caribbean.

"European dancing always has a purpose: to move one's partner, to express the mood of the dancers, to satisfy their love of movement, to entertain them, to intoxicate them and so on. African dance, on the other hand, always has a meaning, a sense. It holds the world order on its course."[10]
(Jahn, pg 85)

Drumming

Beyond its widely known 'secular' functions as a tool of communication or entertainment at public gatherings and events, the drum holds a sacred place in African Spirituality. It is not viewed merely as an instrument of human creation but an Animated Being endowed with a vital force, hence why those used primarily for ritual are first sacralised.

"Generally, African drums are sculpted from a special tree trunk, which must be blessed with an appropriate ritual which varies according to region and society. The wood for drums doesn't warp or give way, regardless of the environment.
However there are drums made out of baked mud, of calabash, and even of metal. The drum may take any shape."[11] (Niangoran-Bouah, pg 82).
It is held that the drum was one of the first instruments created after the Universe and as such the drummer, much like the blacksmith, is highly regarded in traditional African societies.

The drum literally conveys the voice of 'God' and the drummer is key to ensuring that it is the correct message that emanates from the symphonies they play to have the desired result. Little wonder then that it is even found in use during healing rituals for its vibrational frequency and ability to impact on the wellbeing of the diseased individual.
"Drums creates different vibrations and this can actually change the shape of your cells."[12] (Small, 2013)

As touched upon earlier with regards to singing, it is primarily the ability to produce sound, a necessary requirement to traverse realms, which holds it in such high regard.
Even in 'secular' contexts we can witness its power, the audience falling into a trance during a jazz drumming interlude or being compelled to 'bop' their heads and move their bodies in rhythm to the underlying drum pattern.

The role of a drummer as such is a very important one and not to be taken lightly, as one is not simply creating tonal patterns in a sequence, it is way beyond that.

'Drumming is not just bang, bidi bang, each rhythm is perfected in time for a particular reason. In some societies such as the Akan, a drummer of the sacred drums would practice and learn for 40 years before being allowed to play publicly, because the penalty for getting one note wrong could be death. To alter one note is to alter the vibration of the entire symphony.'[13] (Small, 2013)

Meditation & Yoga
Whereas this section might be of surprise to some, it is worthwhile mentioning that what we now generally refer to as 'Meditation' and 'Yoga' are not to found only in Hinduism, Buddhism or the other Eastern practices.
They are many forms of them we see still practised by people of African descent today.

Through advances in Genetic Science, we have irrefutable evidence that human beings originate from Africa, meaning that most things in existence or practice have an African origin. Whilst it can also be argued that some things may be uniquely developed within a certain context or timeframe, it does not disregard the fact that inspiration is usually, always drawn from other things already in existence or that came before.

The landmass we now refer to as India credited with Hinduism is also a region that has been shown to have benefitted from migrations in the past from Kush in Ancient Kemet, where they created the Indus Kush civilisation.

In fact, recent studies (New Scientist, 2008) clearly proves that modern day Indians still carry the genes of their African ancestors. Furthermore, we still have the Jawara people living on the Andaman Islands who still visibly look as African today as

they must have in times past- markedly different to the look typically associated with Indians today.
Wayne Chandler, in his book 'Ancient Futures', highlights this to be the result of the mixture between European colonisers and the African indigenous inhabitants.

We find on some of the walls and papyri of Kemet, visuals showing many of the poses now widely referred to as 'Yoga'. Whilst we have no records in Kemet explicitly referring to them as such, it is not baseless speculation to contend they may well be of an African source.

Especially considering how deeply spiritual they were, like all other African communities, as covered throughout this book, we must ask what other purpose could they serve, apart from a spiritual one?

With meditation practices too, we do not have references explicitly to the use of the breath or emptying of the mind in spiritual development as per Buddhism.
Rather, we have similar practices of sitting still in silence for long periods focussing on water in a calabash or at a flame- as a spiritual development method of 'learning and seeing into the true nature of things'. As is illustrated in the Akan proverb 'Wofwefwe asem mu a, wuhu fwefwe' (One who looks into matter, comprehends it).

Both these practices in the 'East' are associated with the cultivation of 'Kundalini' energy to attain a certain state of spiritual euphoria.
Interestingly, among the Zulu, Credo Mutwa also mentions 'Umbilini' energy- a state also achieved after periods of sitting in silence. For the Khoisan people of Southern Africa also, Umbilini energy is harnessed via a specific ritual dance.

It is, therefore, worth mentioning these two practices in this section as they are not that far removed, in nature or underlying philosophy, from what we now only associate with the 'East'. Even though they exist as slight variations in contemporary practice, their identified purpose(s) are held to be the same, that is, for spiritual development.

Notes

1. Beauvoir, M (2013), Video interview for Ancestral Voices 2 film. Haiti

2. Bempah, K (2014), Video interview for Ancestral Voices 2 film. London

3. Bempah, K (2014), Video interview for Ancestral Voices 2 film. London

4. Small, J (2013), Video interview for Ancestral Voices 2 film. New York

5. Yarborough, C (2013), Video interview for Ancestral Voices 2 film, New York

6. Jahn, J (1961), Muntu: African Culture and the Western World. United States of America: Grove Press Inc. pg 46

7. Some, S (2013), Video interview for Ancestral Voices 2 film. London

8. Yarborough, C (2013), Video interview for Ancestral Voices 2 film, New York

9. Yarborough, C (2013), Video interview for Ancestral Voices 2 film, New York

10. Jahn, J (1961), Muntu: African Culture and the Western World. United States of America: Grove Press Inc. pg 85

11. Niangoran-Bouah in African Traditional Religions in Contemporary Society (1989), edited by Jacob K. Olupona, Georges Paragon House, Minnesota, USA

12. Small, J (2013), Video interview for Ancestral Voices 2 film. New York

13. Small, J (2013), Video interview for Ancestral Voices 2 film. New York

References

Ben-Jochannan, Y.A.A (1991), African Origins of the Major "Western Religions". U.S.A: Black Classic Press

Capone, S (2010), Searching for Africa in Brazil: Power and Tradition in Candomble. U.S.A: Duke University Press.

Chandler, W.B (1999), Ancient Future: The Teachings and Prophetic Wisdom of the Seven Hermetic Laws of Ancient Egypt. United States of America: Black Classic Press

Greber, J (Not provided), Communication with the Spirit World of God: Its Laws and Purpose. UK: Lighting Source UK Ltd.

Jahn, J. (1961), Muntu: African Culture and the Western World. United States of America: Grove Press Inc.

Knappert, J (1990), The Aquarian Guide to African Mythology. England: Thorsons Publishing Group.

Mbiti, J.S (1975), Introduction to African Religion; Second Edition. England: Heinemann Educational Publishers.

Olupona, J.K (1989), African Traditional Religions in Contemporary Society. U.S.A: Paragon House.

Olupona, J.K (2011), African Spirituality: Forms, Meanings & Expressions. U.S.A: The Crossroad Publishing Company.

Chapter 6

Rituals For Living
The means by which one communicates with the spiritual world when consciously awake is through rituals. Rituals are metaphorically, the telecommunications system for accessing the realm beyond the physical.
"Ritual is, above all else, the yardstick by which people measure their state of connection with the hidden ancestral realm, with which the entire community is genetically connected. In a way, the Dagara think of themselves as a projection of the spirit world."[1] (Some M, pg12)

They are as varied in form as they are in purpose and are conducted for a wide range of reasons; thanksgiving for waking in the morning, embarking on journeys and returning safely, successful business transactions, communicating with Forces for guidance and the like.
There are rituals for manifestation, celebrations, grieving, ancestral communication, rites of passage and for cleansing, amongst others.

For every human endeavour or need one can think of, there is a complementary ritual that exists or can be created to meet that need or scenario. Ultimately, it is clear that at the heart of ritual practice is the assertion and recognition of the influence of spirit in our physical lives; they ensure that the relationship between both realms is one that affords balance and favour to the adherent(s).

"The symbolic actions, the libations, invocations, animal sacrifices, fire-baths and so on, in which the possessed take part in a completely conscious state, as well as the states of possession themselves, all serve only to increase the physical and mental powers of man."[2] (Jahn, pg 41)

The word itself as defined by the dictionary implies a prescribed approach to performing a process and whereas this holds true particularly for communal rituals, it is not always the case for individual ones.
Given that human beings are held to be first and foremost Spiritual Beings, there are no restrictions whatsoever on any specific rituals an individual can create and conduct to cater for a personal matter, without any direction from a priest or shaman.

There is no prerequisite for the official priest because the individual is also able to intuit the knowledge or guidance they need on what to do due to their direct connection to the inherent Life Force and their Ancestors' essence within. It is one of the notions that reflects how self-empowering a practice African Spirituality is because the onus is primarily on the individual to tap into this inherent knowledge in becoming, rather than being totally subservient to external powers so to speak.

"Ritual is called for because our soul communicates things to us that the body translates as need, or want, or absence. So we enter into ritual in order to respond to the call of the soul."[3]
(Some, M, pg 25)

Communal rituals
It is at this level of mass ritual practice that the spiritual systems can be perceived as a 'religion' of sorts because all within the community partake of set actions in a collective manner for same objectives.
Such rituals usually mark important events in the life cycle of the community, such as rituals to mark the beginning of a new year, grieving for the passing of community leaders, to mark the start or end of the agricultural season, to cleanse the community of negative entities or to commemorate astronomical events such as a full moon and so on.

Even with these, there is no particular obligation to participate and the individuals can do so of their volition.
However members of the community are generally aware of the importance of participation, not only because of awareness of the power and benefits of collective purpose, but also the adverse effects their non-participation could pose for not just them, but the whole family as a unit within the community.

Rituals are therefore important for social cohesion and collective identity as well as raising awareness of the shared destiny and responsibility to others within the shared community space.
We see an example of this in the Homowo festival celebrated by the Gas of present day Ghana, a celebration at the end of the harvest to give thanks for a good yield and reciprocate this generosity from the Forces of the land.
It consists of many aspects from visits to shrines to appease the divinities, feeding them in return, drumming, dancing and ceremonial processions as well as with the sharing of food between neighbours and others resident in the community or at large.

In Ancient Egypt, the feast of Osiris-Seker-Ptah was an important event in the Calender of the Black Africans during which the Sixth Mystery was celebrated on the 22 of December every year.
During this event was the Feast of the Erection of the Djed Pillar, which symbolised the resurrection of Osiris to maintain stability, law and order.
The reference to it in the Book of the Dead (Coming Forth by Day) declares "Make the word of Orisis truth against his enemies. Raise up the (Djed) which image the resurrection of the god, let the mummy type of the eternal be once more erected as the mainstay and divine support of all."[4] (Walker, pg 40)

Here we discern the use of communal ritual to affect the mind-set and outlook of the entire community, as everyone is invited to envision an immediate future of stability and productivity via visual association with the Djed pillar as an archetype of information.

In this sense, the community is spurred on with a positive outlook to the coming months, reinvigorated in mind and confident of success due to the support of the Neteru.

The family ritual is a communal one but mainly restricted to members of a family. It is usually officiated by the head of the family and can be for the healing, resolution of internal conflicts, or to strengthen the forces of the family shrine to assist with the needs and wants of the family as a whole.

Individual rituals

These refer to those conducted by an individual for a personal need or a group of who have come together united by a purpose. It is such personal practice that can, for lack of a better word, be described as 'magic'.

These can cover offerings to ancestors, Forces of Nature, animal and plant spirits and the like. They open a dialogue between the physical and spiritual, requesting the intervention of other entities to support the adherent(s) in whatever their endeavour.

Rituals can be geared towards the manifestation of the desired objective, or they can be in thanks of achieving them. They can be used to dispel and cleanse the negative energies from others or the environment, to help with the healing of a sick individual or to assist in conception.

The elements used in each particular ritual will vary accordingly and often what is used has symbolic underpinnings tied to the purpose of the ritual.

So for example, rituals which seek the attraction of well-being and wealth could involve the use of honey. The traits of honey associated with 'success' can include its sticky nature, and denotes 'attraction' whilst its sweetness denotes the positive change it will bring in one's life.

We previously covered the use of 'dolls' for women wishing to conceive whereby the wooden doll becomes a symbolic representation of the baby yet to be conceived.

Therefore ritual is not some misguided 'superstitious' action as we have been widely led to believe in the mainstream, nor is it some form of 'devil-worship' either, not forgetting the notion of a being like 'Lucifer' in direct opposition to the Supreme is absent in African Spirituality.

Such similar ideas only came into the spiritual discourses after colonialism, with some early African writers who it would seem, were guided by the notion that the only way to give credibility to their traditional systems was to map each idea in Western Religion(s) with a corresponding African one.

Not surprising, as we do find that most of these early writers such as JB Danquah and Rev J Mbiti were of other religious orientations.

Rather, ritual invites the participants to engage in a high level of psychosomatic exploration of their psyches and inherent capabilities and deep study is required to better identify the components or elements required for conducting an effective ritual. "When one cruises with the world of spirits, rituals are less and less a matter of stopping commotions than they are a matter of maintaining a healthy state of balance. Yet, to arrive at a level of harmony, one must stay in the correct practice of ritual for a lengthy period of time."[5] (Some, M, pg 27)

Aspects of a ritual

All rituals start off with the most important consideration of all- Intent. What is the purpose of the ritual? What does one seek it to resolve or to do?

The intent is the most important aspect of ritual as it effectively determines why a ritual needs to be conducted in the first place. It is likewise the intent that also defines the purpose of the ritual.

Visualisation of the outcome and speaking it into being (invoking it verbally) are also key components understood to help with the manifestation of the desired results. The imagined reality provides the canvas for spirit to draw on in shaping that objective into being.

"Ritual draws from this area of human existence where the spirit plays a life-giving role. We do not make miracles, we speak the kind of language that is interpreted by the supernatural world as a call to intervene in a stabilizing way in a particular life ... We take the initiative to spark a process, knowing that its success is not in our hands but in the hands of the kind of forces we invoke into our lives. So the force field we create within a ritual is something coming from spirit, not something coming from us."[6] (Some, M, pg 32)

A ritual commences with an invocation to the realm of the Ancestors and spirits. It is an occasion approached with humility and respect as one enters the ritual space in need of assistance. There is the recognition that one is trying to achieve an outcome beyond their capability and as such their demeanour has to be reflective of this.

An invocation is made verbally, where a call is put out to specific Ancestors or Forces who are mentioned by name, as a clear invitation to partake in the ritual, as it is their assistance required. Other forms of sounds can also be used to indicate the start of the process and to call in the Spirits such as the ringing of a bell, a cow-bell or the shaking of an asson or maracas to open the portal between worlds so to speak.
It can even be done with pots and pans knocked together to produce the requisite vibrational frequency.

Offerings are provided in respect of the assistance to be given and also to feed and strengthen the essence of the invoked.

It is also a symbolic way of showing appreciation for the work to be done and indicates the reciprocation of favours that will ensue across realms.

After the requests are communicated and the necessary actions performed, such as the pouring of libation, burning of herbs, drinking of medicine, sacrifice of an animal and so on, the spirits are seen off in a respectful manner with thanks given for the assistance they are to provide.
There is/can also be drumming, dancing and singing aspects to a ritual based on the format and number of individuals involved, again for invocation purposes as well as to raise the energy states of the adherents' spirit(s).

The heightened state of such participants can then vibrate in tandem with that of the spirits invoked thereby opening the channel for a union between Life Forces; the phenomenon inaccurately referred to as 'possession'.
The union is a mutual contract between the Life Forces of both the individual and the spirit invoked, whilst the word 'possession' denotes the forcing of one's will on another.
So here again we witness the bane of colonial labelling that seeks to obscure the reality underlining African Spirituality.

The elements that can be included in any ritual are quite limitless; the onus is really on the participants involved regarding what outcomes they would like. So, for instance, some may choose to smudge a space first, as a means of spiritually cleansing it, yet the same can also be achieved by using a broom to sweep the grounds first.

The psyche can also be further heightened with the burning of particular herbs or incense such as frankincense and myrrh.
If a ritual is to offer protection, for instance, an open padlock could be included as a symbolic reference for the open avenue allowing negativity to enter one's life; it is then locked at the end

of the ritual to indicate the closing of said avenue. It can then be buried or placed in a medicinal preparation as a means of spiritually sealing it.

Elements one decides to include in rituals should be carefully considered for their symbolic and functional value in the physical realm as it is reflective of how it will/can then be interpreted spiritually.

Ritual practice is what has been largely used to stigmatise African Spirituality as some form of meaningless practice informed by superstition, yet it is interesting how much of its elements are prevalent in Western Psychology and Sciences, where they are held as 'facts', not 'superstition'.

Authors of best-selling self-help psychology books such as 'Think & Grow Rich', 'The Power of Positive Thinking' and 'The Secret' all espouse the virtues of visualisation and positive thoughts as the foundation for creating the reality one desires.

Athletes train using similar visualisation methods to focus and raise morale for achievement. Writing goals down on paper and burning them as a symbolic way of doing away with negative habits and the like, all reflect similar elements we discern in aspects of African ritual practice.
The same methods are an accepted part of Neuro-Linguistic Programme techniques, so why do we still have the same entrenched negative positions when it comes to African Spirituality?

With Africa being the origin of human consciousness and forms, it follows that such ideas are African in origin. It stands to reason therefore in stating that the 're-formulation' of these principles for the Modern context is just following in the historic tradition of Greek Hermetic re-interpretations of knowledge from the African Mystery Schools of antiquity.

This cannot be denied considering some of these practices, such as the pouring of libation and use of writing to communicate with the immaterial realm, are evidenced in use in the spiritual systems of Ancient Egypt as they still continue now on the continent and its legacy in the Diaspora.

Considering African ritual engages a variety of our senses simultaneously- sounds, smells, vision(s), body movements, verbal invocations- it is clear they provide a more engaging and all-encompassing experience. Far from superstition, were we to even analyse it 'scientifically', the main question to frame such a discussion would be, what happens to all the energy utilised in the ritual?

There is the kinetic energy generated from the drumming, singing and dancing, heat energy generated in the body and mind from the mental projections and invocations and so on. What happens to all this energy generated?

It is only within this Century that Western Scientists, notably Einstein, arrived at the understanding of the conservation and transmutation of energy, 'that it is never destroyed but only changes form'.
So in re-addressing African ritual, it should be immediately clear that it is not only the foods or drinks offered symbolically that are reciprocated in the outcomes we receive but the very energy given off in the process of ritual also partakes in the moulding and shaping of the final results!

Ritual thus provides the human being with the opportunity to exercise the creative power within, by virtue of the 'God'-essence imbued in the human spirit. We enter ritual to become a manifestation of 'God'.

'Witchcraft'/'Sorcery'

With centuries of unchecked discrimination, a word associated with the heinous killings of the Salem Witch hunts and the Spanish Inquisition of America and Europe now almost operates as a synonym to denote the totality of African Spirituality as a system. As a result, it is looked upon as wholly evil; devoid of anything valuable or useful to human progress or development with much fear mongering and ignorance surrounding it.

Terms such as 'Juju' and 'Obeah'- all with negative implications- are used interchangeably with 'Witchcraft' as a synonym for the spiritual system and have contributed to reluctance by the general populace to want to explore or study it in greater detail for better understanding. It has also driven many of its practitioners underground, a situation that fuels the negative use of it as no measures are in place to hold priests or practitioners who may abuse their power to account, unlike what we find for religious organisations such as the Roman Catholic Church.

Witchcraft as a notion solely represents the use of African spiritual principles or rituals for harmful or negative uses.
It represents an attempt to subvert these ideas usually for self-gratification purposes or at the expense of another, causing them damage in the process.
It totally contradicts all the spiritual principles as covered in the first chapter. It does not lend itself to working together for the greater good nor respecting the interconnectedness of things. It seeks the betterment of the individual over or at the expense of the collective.

Even with using these principles in a subservient manner, the individual is acutely aware of the consequent repercussions. As earlier noted, cause and effect is the key operating dynamic within the cosmology, not notions of 'good' and 'bad', as these are open to relative interpretations.

So for the individuals who willingly make the choice to use it adversely, there is the recognition that a similar fate will befall them, one that is of their making.

Following is a collection of rituals shared by various practitioners, shaman and initiates from the complementary film to this book, 'Ancestral Voices: Spirit is Eternal':

Sobonfu Some (Burkina Faso- Dagarra)
An altar in the house is essential as it honours our connection to any spirit we are attracted to and to our ancestors, so a house without an altar is ungrounded.
The mineral kingdom has important qualities of communication to impart to us. From stones to crystals, they are useful in helping us to express ourselves and communicate better, especially for those who tend to be shy. The stones help to record your stories and express yourself better.

They can also be used as decoys for negative energy and certain stones we can wear around our neck help to deflect such energies.

Take a bit of water and pour libation in the morning. Say 'Spirit take this water and make it the river of my life. I don't know where my river is flowing to but I know you do, and so uphold this water and join it with other great rivers out there so my life may flow in a much more smooth way.'
Prayers are, for us, a way to focus our every day's intention so that the purpose for which we are here can manifest

Drink water ritualistically to help bring its healing power into your body, psyche and spirit, to cleanse those parts of your life where healing and cleansing are needed, to bring life into your life. So meditate on what you desire whilst you sip the water so you can call in the healing power of water.

If you feel under constant psychic attack or overloaded with information, you can cover your head with a wrap or hat or keep short hairstyle as our hair acts as antennas that pick up negative energy. Alternatively, you can carry garlic in your pockets as a repellent of negative energy. Keep cups of water with salt in the four corners of a room to use as a means of draining any negative energies in the space. Smudge your home on a daily basis or as often as you feel is necessary.

For those working in a toxic environment, take a bath with some salt, sage, florida water and frankincense as a means to cleanse all the toxic and negative energies you come into contact with daily, due to the environment you find yourself in.

Taking regular conscious walks in Nature is critical to help clear the psyche and free up our psyche and spirit from being stagnant or knotting up. The less contact with Nature we have, the more suffocated we will feel.

Professor Bayyinah Bello (Haiti-Vodou)
Immersing yourself in nature is a great way to learn a lot about what you do not know or even understand, as the direct connection with nature affords a pathway for the transmission and exchange of energy and knowledge, in the form of awareness. So walking barefoot on the land or in water or even getting wet in the rain are great ways to connect with and learn from Nature.

Every morning pour water to the earth in gratitude, three times, with heartfelt compassion as a symbolic means of opening yourself up to be taught by nature as you go around your daily routines.

Credo Mutwa (South Africa- Zulu, Khoisan & Tswana)
Water contains the oldest prayers our minds are capable of. Let us say you want to pray for peace in your country.
Fill your clay vessel with water, lift it up and look into the water, visualise and think of peace, the sounds of birds, the smells of grass- all the beautiful and pleasant things, smells and sounds you can think of and project this into the water.
Then drink half of this water and pour out the rest respectfully onto the ground. Do not spill it in haste or throw it away like rubbish, a sense of reverence must accompany your actions.

Fasting is a ritual we use to bring ourselves closer to the great mind (The Creator). It is referred to as Ukuzila and one must refrain from ingesting any food or other liquids during this time. However one must never deny themselves water during the fast.

You must have special stones in your house. In our tradition, we used to keep special crystals in our huts, as these hold particular qualities that can be used for a range of things- from healing to expanding awareness.

You should have a sacred vessel made of clay or an ostrich's egg. It is primarily to be used in rituals and prayers, particularly for libations.

Using your sacred vessel, half fill it with water and raise it up towards your face. With a happy heart, direct laughter and positivity quietly into the water and wish happiness, strength and peace, or whatever good you intend, towards the person you are praying for. Never, ever, wish someone bad.
You must put the images of what you desire in your head and forgive those people who have done you wrong, then take the water and pour it alternatively on each foot.

Dowoti Desir (Haiti- Vodou)
Altars are in of themselves, seen as an offering to the Ancestors and something as straightforward as placing an image of an ancestor on it is also viewed as an offering to the person.
An altar can be as simple as taking a bookshelf and covering it with a white cloth or a straw mat and placing the picture(s) of deceased family members. It becomes the space where you offer them water, drinks and cigars they liked whilst alive.
All these are manifestations of an offering. Even though you may know some of these things are/were not good for them, you do so because it is ultimately for their enjoyment, not yours.

We can go to the sea, the river or even our backyards and give offerings. We can dig a hole in the ground and pour honey or palm oil in it.

As vessels of the Lwa we are first and foremost, profoundly spiritual beings, so we can pray anytime, anywhere we want. We can wake up and pour libations, you can light a candle any day. This is your way of praying.

We can take special baths we prepare ourselves when we feel the need for such cleansing. We can prepare these baths ourselves by filling it with special herbs, perfumes or flowers, things that carry the essence of what we want to bring into our lives.

Max Beauvoir (Haiti- Vodou)
Its good to have spiritual hygiene and this usually starts with a bath. The best one starts with the inclusion of Nature because remember that 'God' is in all Nature as Nature is in 'God'. Find the proper herbs required and crush these, use alcohol to extract the spirit of the plants and this essence will then also become a part of your skin because you have pores on your skin that allows for this.

In concluding, we can clearly discern that Ritual provides the means through which the individual can exercise their generative power.
It is the means by which we can recognise and tap into inherent 'God' given powers so to speak. Ritual is, therefore, an empowering process, one that provides the opportunity to really learn about and attune with self.

"Spirituality is just like a muscle. The more you do it, the more you develop it, the less you do it, it falls asleep. So if you want to go into spirituality, you have to start practising and you have to reach a point where you give your spiritual life more importance than the physical life because the spiritual life is for ever."[7]
(Bello, 2013)

Notes:

1. Some, M.P (1993), Ritual: Power, Healing, and Community. U.S.A: Penguin Group. Pg 12

2. Jahn, J. (1961), Muntu: African Culture and the Western World. United States of America: Grove Press Inc. pg 41

3. Some, M.P (1993), Ritual: Power, Healing, and Community. U.S.A: Penguin Group. Pg 25

4. Walker, R (2011), Blacks and Religion; Vol 1. UK: Reklaw Education Ltd. Pg 40

5. Some, M.P (1993), Ritual: Power, Healing, and Community. U.S.A: Penguin Group. Pg 27

6. Some, M.P (1993), Ritual: Power, Healing, and Community. U.S.A: Penguin Group. Pg 32

7. Bello, B (2013), Video interview for Ancestral Voices 2 film.

References

Asare Opoku, K. (1978), West African Traditional Religion. Nigeria: FEP International Private Limited.

Bempah, K (2010), Akan Traditional Religion: The Myths and the Truth. Self-published

Dow, C.L (1997), Sarava! Afro-Brazilian Magick. U.S.A: Llewellyn Publications.

Jahn, J. (1961), Muntu: African Culture and the Western World. United States of America: Grove Press Inc.

Okemuyiwa, L.O (2005), Ori The Supreme Divinity. Nigeria: Es-Es Communications Ventures.

Wallis Budge, E.A (1988), Egyptian Magic. England: Penguin Group.

Chapter 7

Recognition & Respect

This is certainly not the first book to attempt to show the unity and correlations in African spiritual philosophy. From Father Tempels' work on 'Bantu Philosophy' (1945) to Jahmein Jahn's 'Muntu' (1961), there have been numerous works that have highlighted the unified philosophies and tenets across all communities since time immemorial.

So the question remains as to why African Spirituality still remains the most misunderstood, vilified and least tolerated of all the faith systems we find in the world today?

The simple answer starts with the scramble and colonisation of Africa first by the Arabs with Islam and then Europeans with Christianity. In a position of power, they could determine what practices were 'lawful' and allowed to be practised.

Those that posed an obstruction to the total subservience of African people were summarily abolished.

Africans who were willing to embrace the religions of their oppressors and reject the spirituality of their Ancestors found social favour via good jobs and placements in senior administrative positions within the colonial establishments.

On the continent and in the Diaspora we have examples of laws being enacted to make traditional systems of veneration a criminal offence- we see this in Haiti, Brasil and the Congo amongst others.

The demonisation of African Spirituality was not just a 'religious' issue; it was also attacked on all fronts in a systematic, institutionalised fashion.

Socially, practitioners were made to look like 'illiterates', 'backward' and 'uncivilised' individuals such that it would carry a social stigma and shame, preventing people from even being interested in preserving their lineage, much less practice it.

These ideas were also infused into the psyche using the educational and political systems as a means of normalising its degradation.

'There is an attempt to paint African spiritual traditions in a negative way and Europeans have produced a whole vocabulary to do it. So when they have a belief system, they are religions, when we have a belief system they are cults.
When they have people ministering their belief systems, they're priests, when we have ours they are shaman or medicine men. When they believe in the subtle forces, its spirituality, when we do its demonology.
Symbols that we use, when they use it, they are symbols when we do they are fetishes. When we have images representing the spiritual forces ours become idols; theirs become icons and we can go on and on with the double standards.'[1] (Walker, 2014)

It is thus understandable why we find people of African descent across the globe today who only publicly identify as Christian or Muslim and lately others- such as Hindu or Buddhist; anything except an African Spiritualist. Yet there is a lot of evidence to suggest that in the direst of circumstances when these foreign religions or medicine has failed the African, they resort to their traditional ways to find a solution- yet this is done clandestinely for fear of sullying their public image.

There are documented reports of many Christian and Muslim clergy, who utilise the powers of the shaman in engaging and keeping their audience, whereas publicly defaming the traditions as 'devil-worship' and so on- blatant hypocrisy at play.

This resistance to African Spirituality by foreign colonisers is also understandable because the main instances where we find people of African descent vehemently resisting their oppression, or even being successful at it has involved the use of traditional knowledge systems.

It remains a source of empowerment to the African and a stumbling block in attempts to secure their total subservience.

We have already highlighted its total success in the Haitian war of liberation. It was a contributing factor to Kimpa Vita being burnt at the stake as a 'witch' by the Catholic Church in the Congo (1706). It was also a driving force behind much of the African wars for Independence- a notable example being in Zimbabwe as its use was more public than in most other African countries.

It also sheds much light on why we do not find it listed in the 'League of World Religions' as an accepted faith practice. Even the various localised names for it, such as Vodun (a national religion in Benin, West Africa), has more followers than required for it to earn a place on this listing and be afforded all the rights and protection its followers deserve, as afforded other religious practitioners.

Using Cuba as an example, Santeria is tolerated to a degree by the Catholic Church whereas Lukumi is not and Palo Mayombe, heavily vilified! The difference?
The degree to which these systems are willing to be 'baptised' and incorporated into the church and how much intermingling it still affords association of African Divinities with Christian saints.

So it would seem that African systems are only socially accepted when or if, they are willing to be appropriated into other systems to gain 'legitimacy'. During periods of active chattel enslavement, it was understandable for Africans to substitute and associate particular deities with saints via certain symbolic signifiers, as the penalty for practising their indigenous systems was death.

Yet even in this current era, without the threat of direct force, it seems some Diasporans are still psychologically attached to the saints and unwilling to let go of them. Thus, Palo Mayombe, which rejected association with the saints is still demonised as 'devil-worship' and 'black magic' whereas Santeria, in Spanish meaning 'The Way of the Saints', is 'respectable' and 'white magic'- apparently only for doing 'good' things.

We see a similar situation in Brasil, where Kandomble is seen as 'dark magic' whereas Umbanda, with its extensive association with European spiritualism, is seen as 'white magic'- the more 'acceptable' of the two.
So the closer the system tries to retain its African identity, the more it is tarred with the same propaganda from colonial times.

It is also worth mentioning how social notions of 'race' and 'class' also plays a role in this stigmatisation of African systems, particularly in the Diaspora. All the systems portrayed as 'evil' seek an 'authentic' African framework, whereas the 'versions' that are deemed 'good' are only made so by the 'blessings' of the same religions that were trying to obliterate African Spirituality less than a thousand years ago.
Perhaps this is also the reason why it is absent from the 'League of World Religions', even the 'versions' deemed 'good', so as to continue to deny it legitimacy in the eyes of the general public.

Why is it important for 'African Spirituality' to be listed?
To end the persecution, abuse and even murders its adherents have to content with the world over, from the Christian to the Muslim world.
The UN and other charities have been reporting on the increase of abuse cases connected to so-called 'witchcraft' or 'sorcery' claims- all words that have now become synonyms for African Spirituality. (Unicef 2010 report on witchcraft abuse in Africa)

This is therefore not just a religious issue anymore, but also a human rights issue- one that must be tackled at a governmental level and addressed on the political playing field. Even with the call for 'Religious Tolerance' post 9/11, traditional African practitioners still await their due.

What has not changed is the utter contempt and disgust it is still met with, even though many people in the main are largely ignorant of what it entails because it has been kept 'in the shadows' for so long.

The aim of this volume has been to show that the term 'African Spirituality' is indeed a valid and accurate label that can be used as an umbrella term to include all the various 'localised' systems. The preceding chapters have evidenced how they are all underpinned by the same principles that consequently influence similar practices; hence there is no valid reason as to why this cannot be done.

The labels 'Christian', 'Muslim', 'Buddhist' are singular terms used to denote religious orientations that likewise are not hegemonic in every sense. Within these terms exist various sects that often do not even exhibit such a wide degree of commonality in philosophy or practice.
So using 'African Spirituality' will also afford similar social, political and institutionalised protection to adherents of this spiritual system across the world.
This is necessary as their persecution is global, often without 'justice' served to the perpetrators or compensation provided for the victims.

On the continent, many parents and communities are abandoning their children at very young ages, some barely nine months old, because some pastor or imam identifies their child to be a 'witch'. In the worst-case scenarios, some of them are even killed.
Women and older women are routinely identified as 'witches' and sent to what are effectively, 'concentration camps', where they are tortured and often sexually abused, to 'confess' and be 'exorcised'.

All this happens with the complicity of many individuals in the higher echelons of the society and so is largely unchecked, even though no credible evidence can be provided that can stand up in a court of law, just opinion and belief.

Similarly in the Diaspora, reports increase year after year of Evangelical Christians especially, persecuting and often murdering African spiritualists in Brasil, the wider Americas and the Caribbean.
This happens even though Kandomble and its variants are recognised as part of the national religions of Brasil after being decriminalised.

What this lack of 'formalisation' does is push the practice(s) underground; leaving them open to exploitation and this is exactly what is happening.
Untrained and uninitiated individuals masquerade as legitimate priests and exploit the fears of their clients, which in turn only feeds the already existing negative representations surrounding these systems.
So it is a double-edged sword regarding the negative effects the lack of official recognition is having on the continued practice of African Spirituality.

It is indeed a sad state of affairs that the singular system from which was birthed all the other mainstream religions of today is still deemed 'evil' is totally irrational; except when understood in a colonising context. It is equally bizarre that for a system constantly painted with negativity, we find absolutely no historical evidence of its use in the pillage or conquer of others.

No recorded acts of going to war or invading others, committing genocide and other heinous crimes all in the name of an African 'God', whereas other sanctioned belief systems claiming to be about 'peace' and 'love' are responsible for some of the worst atrocities and genocides in human history.
Yet the African 'God' or Creator is still largely associated with the concept of the 'Devil' as found in the Abrahamic faiths- another

colonial hangover that continues to plague spiritual practitioners and skew understandings.

We can understand this state of affairs by examining the cosmological principles informing African Spirituality as has been outlined all throughout this book. It is an inclusive system that recognises and respects all beings, whether salient or not, based on the Vital Force present within all.

It further explains why there are no forced 'conversions' or 'evangelism' either- after all, how can one convert 'God' back to 'God'? If we all share the same Life Force from the same source, then how can one direct another back to that same source simply through dogma and man-made rules?

'In Africa, we don't build shrines to our God, we build shrines to the qualities and attributes of God. We don't even have images of God 'cos we say no one knows what God looks like. If God is every and all things at once if God is all of creation at once, then how can you have a picture of God hanging on your wall? How can you fit all of creation into a picture?'[2] (Small, 2013)

A system where justice is swift and fair, as the balance must always prevail, without recourse to 'exempt passes' such as repentance, or being remorseful, thereby encouraging ownership and responsibility for actions.

A system where there is no need for an incentive as reward for good behaviour, but rather the understanding that such actions are necessary if one is to develop into their full abilities and power.

A system that encourages ecologically-sound living and respect for the environment thereby affording sustainable human development- crucial in this time of scarcity due to over-exploitation of the world's resources.

A system that embodies inclusivity as an essential fundamental principle of living, encouraging respect and consideration for all beings, salient and non-salient, very necessary at this time of global religious strife and intolerance.

Are we still going to continue to turn a blind eye to the world's oldest faith practice when it has so much to offer us- just because of untruths made up to sustain an Imperialistic agenda that has only ended up dividing and throwing the world into chaos?

In doing so we continue to do ourselves an injustice, as much could be learnt from an in-depth exploration of African Spirituality- from the fields of medicine to eco-living.
We have already covered a few areas that show clearly that the African was millennia ahead in their understandings of psychosomatic processes.

However, the foreign invaders could not comprehend the essence of African Cosmologies at the time and it had to take centuries of scientific exploration to 'discern' the same concepts and then claim them as 'new discoveries'. Will we confine ourselves to the same myopic vision of yesteryear in this current era?

Or will we submit to listening to the wisdom of the Ancestors who had the benefit of millennia of observations to deeply understanding the workings of the spirit, body, mind, our world, the universe and our place(s) within it?

'Sankofa, we have to pull from the back what made us strong and use it right now. We have to change, we have to grow, we have to acknowledge different philosophical approaches to life and redo ourselves. What did the ancient teachings say? Know yourself. Don't run from being African, don't run from the African story, it's the greatest story that could be told. Know yourself and re-create yourself.'[3] (Yarborough, 2013)

Notes

1. Walker, R (2014), Video interview for Ancestral Voices 2 film, London.

2. Small, J (2013), Video interview for Ancestral Voices 2 film, New York.

3. Yarborough, C (2013), Video interview for Ancestral Voices 2 film, New York.

3. Unicef (April 2010), Children Accused of Witchcraft: An anthropological study of contemporary practices in Africa. PDF file accessed 20/02/2016

http://www.unicef.org/wcaro/wcaro_children-accused-of-witchcraft-in-Africa.pdf

BIBLIOGRAPHY

Jahn, J. (1961), Muntu: African Culture and the Western World. United States of America: Grove Press Inc.

Wallis Budge, E.A (1988), Egyptian Magic. England: Penguin Group.

Dow, C.L (1997), Sarava! Afro-Brazilian Magick. U.S.A: Llewellyn Publications.

Quarcoopome, T.N.O (1987), West African Traditional Religion. Nigeria: African Universities Press

Opoku Asare, K (1978), West African Traditional Religion. Nigeria: FEP International Private Limited.

Ben-Jochannan, Y.A.A (1991), African Origins of the Major "Western Religions". U.S.A: Black Classic Press

Greber, J (Not provided), Communication with the Spirit World of God: Its Laws and Purpose. UK: Lighting Source UK Ltd.

Knappert, J (1990), The Aquarian Guide to African Mythology. England: Thorsons Publishing Group.

Mutwa, V.C (1996), Zulu Shaman: Dreams, Prophecies and Mysteries. U.S.A: Lakebook Manufacturing Inc.

Lartey, E.Y.A (2013), Postcolonializing God. UK: SCM Press.

Umeh, J.A (1999), After God is Dibia; Vol 1. Britain: Karnak House.

Umeh, J.A (1999), After God is Dibia; Vol 2. Britain: Karnak House.

Some, M.P (1994), Of Water and the Spirit. U.S.A: Penguin Group.

Etefa, T (2012), Integration and Peace in East Africa. U.S.A: Palgrave Macmillan.

Voeks, R.A (1997), Sacred Leaves Of Candomble. U.S.A: University of Texas Press.

Gonzalez-Wippler, M (1989), Santeria The Religion. U.S.A: Llewellyn Worldwide.

Okemuyiwa, L.O (2005), Ori The Supreme Divinity. Nigeria: Es-Es Communications Ventures.

Danquah, J.B (1944), The Akan Doctrine of God; Second Ed. England: Routledge

Mason, J (2003), Who's Knocking on my Floor?: Esu Arts in the Americas. Yoruba Theological Archministry.

Asante, M.K & Mazama, A (2009), Encyclopedia of African Religion; Vol 2. U.S.A: Sage Publications.

Some, M.P (1993), Ritual: Power, Healing, and Community. Penguin Group.

Fu-Kiau, K.K.B (1980), African Cosmology of the Bantu-Kongo: Principles of Life & Living. Canada: Athellia Henrietta Press.

MacGaffey, W (1986), Religion and Society in Central Africa. U.S.A: The University of Chicago Press.

Mbiti, J.S (1975), Introduction to African Religion; Second Edition. England: Heinemann Educational Publishers.

Olupona, J.K (1989), African Traditional Religions in Contemporary Society. U.S.A: Paragon House.

Capone, S (2010), Searching for Africa in Brazil: Power and Tradition in Candomble. U.S.A: Duke University Press.

Morodenibig, N.N.L (2011), Philosophy Podium: A Dogon Perspective; Second Edition. U.S.A: Firefly Productions.

Olupona, J.K (2011), African Spirituality: Forms, Meanings & Expressions. U.S.A: The Crossroad Publishing Company.

Ephirim-Donkor, A (1997), African Spirituality: On becoming Ancestors. Eriteria: Africa World Press Inc.

Bempah, K (2010), Akan Traditional Religion: The Myths and the Truth. Self-published

Tempels, P (2010), Bantu Philosophy. U.S.A: HBC Publishing.

Neimark, P.J (1993), The Way of the Orisa. U.S.A: HarperCollins.

Mbiti, J (1970), African Religions and Philosophy. U.S.A: Anchor Books.

Amen, R.U.N (1990), Metu Neter; Vol 1. U.S.A: Kharmit Media Trans Visions Inc.

Amen, R.U.N (2008), Metu Neter; Vol 3. U.S.A: Kharmit Media Trans Visionos Inc.

Rankin, A (2010), Many-Sided Wisdom: A new politics of the spirit. UK: O Books.

Stone, M (1976), When God was a Woman. U.S.A: Harcourt Brace & Company.

Thompson, R.F (1983), Flash of the Spirit; African & Afro-American Art & Philosophy. U.S.A: First Vintage Books Edition.

Walker, R (2011), Blacks and Religion; Vol 1. UK: Reklaw Education Ltd.

Dieterlien, G & Griaule, M (1986), The Pale Fox. France: Continuum Foundation.

For More Information:
www.ancestralvoices.co.uk

Notes

Made in the USA
Charleston, SC
14 September 2016